GRILLED COOKBOOK

Best-ever Bbq and Grilling Cookbook for Beginners (A Bbq and Grilling Cookbook for Effortless Meals)

Larry Jarvis

Published by Sharon Lohan

© Larry Jarvis

All Rights Reserved

Grilled Cookbook: Best-ever Bbq and Grilling Cookbook for Beginners (A Bbq and Grilling Cookbook for Effortless Meals)

ISBN 978-1-990334-79-5

All rights reserved. No part of this guide may be reproduced in any form without permission in writing from the publisher except in the case of brief quotations embodied in critical articles or reviews.

Legal & Disclaimer

The information contained in this book is not designed to replace or take the place of any form of medicine or professional medical advice. The information in this book has been provided for educational and entertainment purposes only.

The information contained in this book has been compiled from sources deemed reliable, and it is accurate to the best of the Author's knowledge; however, the Author cannot guarantee its accuracy and validity and cannot be held liable for any errors or omissions. Changes are periodically made to this book. You must consult your doctor or get professional medical advice before using any of the suggested remedies, techniques, or information in this book.

Table of contents

PART 1 1

VEGGIE GRILLED SANDWICH CALIFORNIA STYLE 2

PITA PIZZA 4

PORTOBELLO MUSHROOM BURGERS 5

BLACK BEAN VEGGIE BURGER 6

GRILLED POTATOES AND ONION 7

VEGGIE GRILLED PIZZA 8

TOFU WITH RATATOUILLE, GRILLED 11

GRILLED VEGETABLE SALAD 13

TOFU STEAKS WITH GINGER & SESAME 14

GRILLED VEGETABLE LASAGNA 15

GRILLED RECIPES 17

1. DELICIOUS PIZZA GRILLED CHEESE 18

2. AMAZING GRILLED CHEESE WITH CARAMELIZED ONIONS 20

3. AMAZING NACHO ABUELITOS GRILLED CHEESE 22

4. AMAZING FONTINA AND MOZZARELLA GRILLED CHEESE WITH BACON, HONEY AND APPLES 24

5. WONDERFUL TOMBSTONE AND COFFIN GRILLED CHEESES 26

6. DELICIOUS GRILLED TWO-CHEESE BURGERS WITH GARLIC DRESSING 28

7. AMAZING ADRIATIC 30

8. HEALTHY ALPINE 32

9. HEALTHY AMELIA 34

10. WONDERFUL ATHENA 36

11. DELICIOUS BACON HABANERO 38

12. AMAZING BENEDICT 40

13. AMAZING TEX 42

14. AMAZING BUFFALO BILL 44

15. DELICIOUS CHARLOTTE 46

16. WONDERFUL DELILAH 48

17. RHUBARB AND BAKED AVOCADO 49

18. GRILLED CHEESE SANDWICH 52

19. DELICIOUS PICO DE GALLO GRILLED CHEESE SANDWICH 53

20. DELICIOUS GRILLED CHEESE DE MAYO 55

21. TASTY GRILLED CHEESE SANDWICH 56

22. DELICIOUS GRILLED CHEESE, CINNAMON, AND APPLE SANDWICH 57

23. TASTY BACON, AVOCADO, AND PEPPER JACK GRILLED CHEESE SANDWICH 58

24. DELICIOUS GRILLED CHEESE WITH GOUDA, ROASTED MUSHROOMS AND ONIONS 59

25. AMAZING MEDITERRANEAN GRILLED CHEESE SANDWICH 61

26. AMAZING GREEN GODDESS GRILLED CHEESE SANDWICH 63

27. HEALTHY BALSAMIC BLUEBERRY GRILLED CHEESE SANDWICH 65

28. TASTY HAWAIIAN GRILLED CHEESE 67

29. HEALTHY GRILLED CHEESE ROLLS 68

30. AMAZING AVOCADO-GREEN-RED-GRATED CHEESE-SLICED BREAD 69

31. HEALTHY BEET, ARUGULA & GOAT CHEESE GRILLED CHEESE 71

32. CORNED BEEF WITH MUSTARD AND CHEESE 73

33. DELICIOUS ROASTED TOMATO SOUP WITH GRILLED CHEESE CROUTONS 75

34. DELICIOUS GRILLED CHEESE CROUTONS: 77

35. AMAZING GRILLED CHEESE WITH GOUDA, ROASTED MUSHROOMS AND ONIONS 78

PART 2 80

INTRODUCTION 81

CHICKEN SATAY WITH SPICY PEANUT SAUCE 83

CHICKEN SHISH KABOBS 86

FLAME-GRILLED STEAK 89

FLAME-GRILLED BEEF BURGERS 91

GRILLED CHICKEN DRUMSTICK WITH ROSEMARY 93

GRILLED CUMIN LAMB CHOPS 95

SPICED LAMB SKEWERS 97

GRILLED LEMON BUTTER SHRIMP 99

SPICY GRILLED SHRIMP 102

GRILLED RACK OF LAMB WITH MIXED HERBS 104

GRILLED SCALLOPS WITH GARLIC AND SCALLIONS 106

GRILLED SEAFOOD ON SKEWERS 108

GRILLED TROUT WITH ONION AND HERBS 110

GRILLED TUNA BELLY WITH DILL 112

PEANUT MARINATED CHICKEN SATAY 114

GRILLED STEAK WITH HOMEMADE BALSAMIC MARINADE 116

GRILLED BEEF SKEWERS WITH INDIAN SPICE MARINADE 118

GRILLED CHILI LIME CHICKEN KEBABS 121

HOMEMADE JERK CHICKEN DRUMSTICK 124

EASY GRILLED RIB EYE 127

GRILLED ITALIAN SALMON STEAKS 130

HONEY MUSTARD GRILLED CHICKEN	132
GRILLED KOREAN CHICKEN WINGS	134
GRILLED LAMB CHOPS WITH WHOLEGRAIN MUSTARD	136
GRILLED CHICKEN LEGS	138
GRILLED MUSSELS WITH BASIL PESTO	140
CHICKEN SAUSAGE-FILLED SQUID SKEWERS	142
BEEF SKEWERS WITH TERIYAKI SAUCE	145
KOREAN-STYLE RIB BBQ	147
MARINATED GRILLED SHRIMP	150
GRILLED BEEF BRATWURST	153
ULTIMATE CHICKEN BARBECUE	155
SPICY GRILLED STEAKS	157
CHIPOTLE GARLIC LAMB CHOPS	160
EASY GRILLED SQUID	162
CITRUS-MARINATED GRILLED CHICKEN BREASTS	164
GRILLED LAMB CHOPS WITH HERBS	166
SHISH KABOBS	168
GRILLED SALMON WITH LEMON AND THYME	170
SPICY GRILLED LOBSTER	172
SWEET AND SPICY GRILLED TUNA BELLY	174
SPICED SHRIMP SKEWERS WITH GARLIC AND HERB	176
HOMEMADE GRILLED PIZZA	178
GRILLED VEGETABLES WITH HERBS	181
GRILLED CARROT AND ASPARAGUS	184
EASY CORN KABOBS	187

GRILLED MIXED VEGGIES **189**

Part 1

Veggie Grilled Sandwich California Style

Ingredients:

Lemon juice (a tbsp)
Mayonnaise (quarter a cup)
Minced garlic (3 cloves)
Oilve oil (1/8 cup)
Red bell peppers, sliced (a cup)
Sliced small zucchini (1 piece)
Sliced red onion (1 piece)
Small yellow squash, sliced (a piece)
Foccacia bread pieces sliced horizontally
Feta cheese, crumbled (1/2 cup)

Directions:

Make the marinade: Take a cup and mix the garlic, lemon juice and mayonnaise. Chill in refrigerator until needed.

Prepare the vegetables by brushing each side with olive oil. Lay the zucchini and bell peppers on the grill right in the middle, surrounded by the onions and squash. Cook the vegetables for around 3 min before turning and cooking for additional 3 min. Move away from grill to put aside until needed.

Spread the mayonnaise mixture on the cut sides of the foccacia bread before sprinkling with feta cheese. Place on the grill, with the cheese side up, and grill with cover for 2 to 3 minutes.

Remove from grill when cheese is slightly melted and layer with vegetables, making for open-faced sandwiches.

Pita Pizza

Ingredients:

Pita bread (1 round)
Olive oil (1 tsp)
Pizza sauce (3 tbsp)
Shredded mozzarella cheese (1/2 cup)
Sliced crimini mushrooms (1/4 cup)
Garlic salt (1/8 tsp)

Directions:

Spread one side of the pita bread with olive oil and pizza sauce before topping with cheese and mushrooms and sprinkling with garlic salt.
Place pita pizza on a preheated grill and cook with the lid until cheese melts which is about 5 minutes.

Portobello Mushroom Burgers

Ingredients:

Portobello mushroom caps (4 mushrooms)
Balsamic vinegar (1/4 cup)
Olive oil (2 tbsp)
Dried basil (1 tsp)
Dried oregano (1 tsp)
Minced garlic (1 tbsp)
Salt and pepper to taste
Provolone cheese (1 ounce x 4 slices)

Directions:

In a shallow dish, place mushroom caps, smooth side up. In another bowl, mix together the vinegar, basil, oil, oregano, salt, garlic and pepper. Pour this mixture over the mushrooms and let stand for 15 minutes turning over twice.
Place the mushrooms on a preheated grill, setting aside the marinade for basting. Grill the mushrooms for about 5 to 8 minutes or until tender. Baste with marinade frequently, topping with cheese during the last 3 minutes of grilling.

Black Bean Veggie Burger

Ingredients:

Drained and rinsed black beans (16 ounce x 1 can)
Green bell pepper cut into ½ inch pieces (1/2 cup)
Onion cut into wedges (1/2 cup)
Peeled garlic (3 cloves)
1 egg
Chili powder (1 tbsp)
Cumin (1 tbsp)
Thai chili sauce or hot sauce (1 tsp)
Bread crumbs (1/2 cup)

Directions:

Mash black beans with a fork or masher until thick in a medium bowl.
In a food processer, chop bell pepper, garlic and onion before stirring into mashed beans.
In a separate bowl, stir together chili powder, egg, chili sauce and cumin.
Stir the egg mixture into the mashed beans before adding bread crumbs. Mix until the mixture holds together before dividing into patties.
Place patties on foil before grilling on a preheat grill for about 8 minutes on each side.

Grilled Potatoes and Onion

Ingredients:

Sliced potatoes (4 pieces)
Sliced red onion (1 piece)
Salt (1 tsp)
Ground black pepper (1 tsp)
Butter (4 tbsp)

Directions:

Place some potatoes and onion in the center of 2 or 3 squares of aluminum foil. Season with salt and pepper and a dot of butter. Wrap this with the edges of aluminum foil making into a flattened square before sealing the edges. Repeat all of this with remaining vegetables.
Place aluminum wrapped package over a preheated grill, cook for about 30 minutes turning only once. Serve immediately after cooking.

Veggie Grilled Pizza

Ingredients:

Olive oil, divided (10 tsp)
Warm water (1 cup)
Bread flour (10 ounce)
Baker's yeast, dry (around 2 tsp)
Salt-kosher, divided (1 tsp)
Cooking spray
Yellow cornmeal (2 tbsp)
Small eggplant in slices of about about an inch thick (12 ounces)
Zucchini in slices cut across and about an inch thick(1 piece)
Bell pepper cut in four parts and seeded (1 piece)
Minced garlic (3 cloves)
Pizza Sauce, standard (2/3 cup)
Black pepper, grinded (1/4 tsp)
Fontina cheese, grated (a cup x 4 ounces)
Mint, fine leaves (a quater cup)
Thyme, fresh blades (2 tsp)

Preparation:

Take a large mixing bowl and pour ¾ cup of the readied warm water. Gradually put flour in the bowl to mix it with the water. Cover and wait for 20 minutes. Meanwhile, combine the yeast with the rest of the water in a smaller bowl and let stand until bubbles appear. Put ½ tsp salt, 4 tsp oil and the dissolved yeast to flour mixture and mix until the dough gets ready.

Put dough in another larger bowl and smear with cooking spray before tightly wrapping with plastic smeared with more cooking spray. Then leave the dough in the fridge for 24 hours. Take it out and begin to pound it down. Form the dough as an oval, of at least 12-inches using a slightly floured baking sheet powdered with cornmeal. Form a border by crimping the edges and use a plastic wrap to slightly cover the dough.

Brush vegetables with the rest of the oil (2 tbs). Cook eggplant on the grill until tender and set aside in a dish. Zucchinis need to be grilled for 3 min, turning the sides and then add it to the eggplant. Cook the pepper quarters on the grill, placing skin side down and until blisters appear. Let stand in a sealed bag for a few minutes before peeling the skin and adding to the combination of vegetables. Chop vegetables. Now add garlic and toss to mix.

Coat the dough with cooking spray, place on the grill turning up the cornmeal side and keep until blisters appear. Change the dough side on the grill and keep for another 3 min. Take away from grill and daub the surface of the crust with the sauce for pizza leaving a border. Place an even layer of vegetable mixture over sauce and evenly spice with black pepper and salt. Put cheese on the top before returning pizza unto the grill and cook for another 4 min or until cheese is melted. Dredge with the rest of the spices (mint and thyme).

Tofu with Ratatouille, Grilled

Ingredients:

Organic vegetable broth (1 cup)
Fresh orange juice (1/2 cup)
Dry rosé wine (1/2 cup)
Dried herbes de Provence (2 tsp)
Olive oil (2 tbsp)
Olive paste (1 tbsp)
Kosher salt (1/2 tsp)
Freshly ground black pepper (1/4 tsp)
Minced garlic (4 cloves)
Extra-firm tofu, cut into 8 slices (14-ounce x 1 package)
Small eggplants cut lengthwise into 4 slices (3 pieces)
Small zucchini cut lengthwise into 4 slices (3 pieces)
Sweet onion cut into 1/2-inch-thick slices (1 piece)
1 large red bell pepper, cut into 8 wedges
Small tomatoes (4 piecces)
Cooking spray
Chopped fresh basil (2 tbsp)
Chopped fresh parsley (1 tbsp)
Chopped fresh thyme (1 tbsp)

Preparation:

Place first 4 ingredients in a saucepan over medium heat and bring to a boil. Cook until slightly thick and reduce to 1/3 cup, which takes about 10 minutes.

Remove from heat and stir in olive oil and the next 4 ingredients (until garlic).

Place vegetables and tofu on a grill coated with cooking spray. Brush half of the juice mixture over the vegetables and tofu and grill for about 4 minutes. Turn them over and brush with more juice mixture and cook for another 3 minutes.

Combine parsley, basil and thyme. Sprinkle this herb mixture over the tofu and vegetables.

Grilled Vegetable Salad

Ingredients:

Plum or heirloom tomatoes (4 pieces)
1 medium Zucchini cut lengthwise into 4 slices (1 tbsp)
Yellow squash cut lengthwise into 4 slices (2 pieces)
Baby eggplants cut into 4 pieces (2 pieces)
Red bell pepper, seeded and cut into wedges (2 pieces)
Red onion cut into thick slices (2 pieces)
Asparagus (1 pound)
Olive oil (2 tbsp)
Salt (1/2 tsp)
Mixed salad greens (6 cups)
Pistachio vinaigrette
Crumbled goat cheese

Preparation:

Combine vegetables onto a bowl and drizzle with olive oil before seasoning with salt and pepper.
Grill vegetables about 5 to 6 minutes on each side. Cut vegetables into bite-size pieces.
Toss salad greens with ¼ cup of the vinaigrette and place vegetables on greens before sprinkle with goat cheese. Serve with the rest of the vinaigrette.

Tofu Steaks with Ginger & Sesame

Ingredients:

Extra-firm tofu crosswise into 8 slices (1 pound)
Ginger-Sesame Vinaigrette (2/3 cup)
Finely chopped fresh cilantro (1 tbsp)
Low-sodium soy sauce (1 tbsp)
Lime (8 slices)
Cooking spray
Cooked white rice (2 cups)

Preparation:

Place tofu on several paper towels before covering with more additional paper towels. Let stand for 20 minutes and pressing down occasionally. Combine vinaigrette, soy sauce and cilantro in a baking dish. Remove ¼ of that mixture and set aside. Add tofu onto the baking dish in a single layer, turning to coat evenly. Cover and marinate in fridge for about 30 minutes, turning occasionally.
Add the lime to the marinade. Remove the tofu, reserve the marinade. Place tofu and lime slices on grill grate coated with cooking spray and cook for 2 minutes on each side.
Spoon ½ cup rice onto 4 plates. Top servings with tofu slices and lime slices, drizzling servings with 1 tbsp with cilantro mixture.

Grilled Vegetable Lasagna

Ingredients:

3 eggplants sliced to ¼ inch thick slices (about 3 pounds)
3 zucchini cut into 1/8-inch slices (about 1 1/4 pounds)
Cooking spray
Salt, divided (1 tsp)
Freshly ground black pepper, divided (3/4 tsp)
Red bell peppers quarter and seeded (2 pieces)
Fat-free ricotta cheese (1 (15-ounce) container)
1 egg
Grated Asiago cheese, divided (3/4 cup)
Minced fresh basil (1/4 cup)
Minced fresh parsley (1/4 cup)
Lasagna noodles, divided (9 pieces)
Tomato-basil spaghetti sauce, divided (1 (26-ounce) jar)
Shredded part-skim mozzarella cheese, divided (3/4 cup (about 3 ounces))
Commercial pesto (1/4 cup)

Preparation:

Coat zucchini and eggplants with cooking spray and sprinkle with ¼ tsp pepper and ½ tsp salt before grilling the vegetables about 1 ½ minute on each side or until tender. Let cool and combine in a large bowl.

Grill the bell peppers for about 3 minutes or until tender before cutting into 1-inch strips. Add these with the eggplants mixture.

Combine egg, ricotta and ½ Asiago cheese, parsley, basil and ½ tsp each of salt and pepper.

Cook the lasagna noodles according to package directions. Preheat the oven 375 degrees F.

Spread ½ cup of the spaghetti sauce in the bottom a baking dish coated with cooking spray. Arrange at least 3 noodles over the sauce. Top with half of the eggplant mixture before spreading half of the cheese mixture. Sprinkle with ¼ cup of mozzarella cheese. Repeat this process until the baking dish is full.

Spoon the remaining spaghetti sauce over the noodles before sprinkling with remaining cheeses and baking for 1 hour. Let stand for at least 15 minutes before serving.

Grilled recipes

1. Delicious Pizza Grilled Cheese

Ingredients

- 1 cup ricotta
- 2 cups shredded mozzarella, plus for decorating
- 1 1/4 cups freshly grated Parmesan
- 1/2 cup diced pepperoni, plus 12 large slices and 4 slices for garnish
- 2 tablespoons chopped fresh basil
- 6 tablespoons butter, at room temperature
- 12 slices rustic white bread
- 3/4 cup jarred marinara sauce, plus more for dipping, optional
- 36 black olive slices
- 18 green olive slices

Method

1. Preheat the oven to 425 degrees F.
2. In a medium bowl, using a rubber spatula, mix together the ricotta, mozzarella, 1/2 cup of the Parmesan, the diced pepperoni and the basil until well combined.
3. Butter one side of each slice of bread. Working buttered side down, spread each slice with 1 tablespoon of the marinara. Divide the cheese mixture

among 6 slices of the bread, and sandwich with the remaining slices. For each sandwich, sprinkle the top piece of bread with 1 tablespoon of the remaining Parmesan. Flip, and sprinkle the other side with an additional tablespoon of Parmesan.

4. To make all of these sandwiches at once, heat 2 baking pans in the oven for 10 minutes. Spray the bottom of one of the pans with cooking spray, and place the buttered and Parmesan-ed sandwiches in the pan. Spray the underside of the second pan, and place it on top of the sandwiches. Bake until golden brown and crispy, and the cheese is melted, 10 minutes.

5. Cut each sandwich into 3 pieces. Using a few shreds of mozzarella cheese as glue, make a face using the black olive slices as eyes, the green olive slices as a nose, and the pepperoni slices as a mouth. Melt for 4 minutes in the oven to adhere.

6. Serve with marinara for dipping if desired.

2. Amazing Grilled Cheese with Caramelized Onions

Ingredients

- 2 tablespoons canola oil
- 5 tablespoons unsalted butter, softened
- 2 large onions, sliced
- 2 teaspoons sherry vinegar
- 1 teaspoon sugar
- 12 slices rustic Italian bread (each about 1/2-inch thick)
- 8 ounces Gruyere, thinly sliced

Method

1. Heat the canola oil and 1 tablespoon butter in a large saute pan over medium heat. When the butter is melted, add the onions and cook, stirring occasionally, until dark brown and caramelized, about 25 minutes. Add the vinegar, sugar and 2 tablespoons water, scrapping up any dark bits that have accumulated on the bottom of the pan. Continue to cook until all the liquid has evaporated. Transfer the onions to a bowl and reserve.

2.   Butter 1 side of each bread slice. Lay 6 slices butter-side down on a work surface. Top each with 2 slices of Gruyere, a dollop of the onions and 2 more slices of Gruyere. Top with another slice of bread, butter-side up.

3.   Heat a cast-iron griddle over medium heat. Add the sandwiches and cook until the cheese begins to melt and the bread is golden brown, 2 to 4 minutes. Flip and continue to cook until golden brown and the cheese is melted through, 2 to 4 minutes. Cut in half and serve immediately.

3. Amazing Nacho Abuelitos Grilled Cheese

Ingredients

- 1 tablespoon vegetable oil
- 1 pound ground fresh Mexican chorizo
- 8 slices good quality white bread, such as Arnold Country White Sliced
- 8 ounces shredded Chihuahua cheese
- 1/2 cup sliced black olives
- 1/4 cup pickled jalapenos, sliced
- 4 tablespoons salted butter, softened
- Honey Chipotle Crema:
- 1 cup sour cream
- 1 tablespoon chopped fresh cilantro
- 1 tablespoon honey or agave
- 1 chipotle pepper in adobo, minced
- 1/2 lime, juiced
- Kosher salt and pepper

Method

1. In a large skillet, heat the vegetable oil and brown the chorizo over medium heat until cooked through, about 8 minutes. Using a slotted spoon, scoop

out the chorizo, and move to a paper-towel-lined plate. Set aside.

2. In between two pieces of bread, layer the cheese, chorizo, olives, jalapenos and then another layer of cheese. Add some butter to the griddle over medium-low heat, and place the sandwich on the griddle. Add more butter to the top of the bread and cover with a metal bowl until golden on the outside and gooey in the middle, 5 minutes per side. Open the sandwich and place a few tortilla chips inside, then close again.

3. Cut into quarters, serve with a side of Honey Chipotle Crema, and be prepared to never eat conventional nachos again.

4. Honey Chipotle Crema:

5. Mix the sour cream, cilantro, honey, chipotle pepper, lime juice and some salt and pepper together, and set aside.

4. Amazing Fontina and Mozzarella Grilled Cheese with Bacon, Honey and Apples

Ingredients

- 12 slices bacon
- 8 slices fresh mozzarella, 1/4 inch thick
- 8 slices pumpernickel
- 1 stick unsalted butter, at room temperature
- 1/4 cup Dijon mustard
- 16 slices fontina, thinly sliced from the deli
- 1 Honey Crisp apple, peeled and sliced really thinly

Method

1. Cook the bacon in a large saute pan over medium heat until brown and crispy on both sides. Transfer to a plate lined with paper towels and reserve.
2. Preheat a griddle or nonstick saute pan to medium. Between two pieces of paper towels, pat dry the mozzarella.
3. Spread each piece of bread with a thin, even layer of butter. Spread the other side of each piece of

bread with Dijon. Lay the bread down with the Dijon sides facing up on a baking sheet.

4. Place one slice of fontina, one slice of mozzarella and then another slice of fontina on each piece of bread. Lay 3 bacon slices on half of the slices of the cheese-lined bread. Top the bacon with an even layer of apple slices (these are the bottoms, the ones with just cheese are the tops--together they make a pair!).

5. Place the tops and bottoms on the griddle butter-side down and cook until the bread gets brown and crusty and the cheese begins to melt, 5 to 7 minutes. When the cheese is nice and melty, flip the tops onto the bottoms so the cheese is on the inside. Give each sandwich a press, flip over and cook for 1 to 2 minutes more.

6. Cut the sandwiches in half on the bias and serve hot.

5. Wonderful Tombstone and Coffin Grilled Cheeses

Ingredients

- 1 cup shredded sharp Cheddar
- 1 cup shredded Gouda
- 1 cup shredded mozzarella
- 1 cup shredded Monterey Jack
- 8 slices white sandwich bread (preferably the kind that has a bit of a heart shape on the top)
- 1/4 cup prepared pesto
- 8 slices dark sandwich bread, such as pumpernickel or rye
- 1/4 cup fig jam
- 1 stick (8 tablespoons) unsalted butter, melted
- 1/2 cup ketchup in a squeeze bottle
- 1/2 cup mustard in a squeeze bottle
- 8 cups thinly shredded iceberg lettuce (about 1 head)

Method

1. Preheat the oven to 450 degrees F.
2. Toss together the Cheddar, Gouda, mozzarella and Monterey Jack in a medium bowl. Lay the white

bread on a work surface and spread the pesto evenly on half the slices. Spread half the cheese mixture (about 1/4 cup per sandwich) on the bread with the pesto and top with the remaining white bread to make 4 sandwiches; place on a parchment-lined baking sheet.

3. Lay the dark bread on the work surface and spread the fig jam evenly on half the slices. Use the remaining cheese mixture and bread to make 4 sandwiches. Add the sandwiches to the baking sheet. Brush both sides of the white bread and dark bread sandwiches with melted butter. Bake for 5 minutes, then flip and bake for 3 minutes more.

4. Make the tombstones: Cut the crusts off the sides and curved tops of the white bread sandwiches, following the curves of the tops. Leave the bottom crusts on. Next, cut each sandwich in half lengthwise so that the pieces resembles tombstones.

5. Make the coffins: Cut the crusts off 3 sides of each sandwich, leaving 1 short side uncut. Halve each sandwich crosswise to make 2 long rectangles. Leaving a flat edge on the top and bottom of the short sides of each rectangle, make diagonal cuts at each corner to create a long hexagonal coffin shape. Add spooky decorations to the tombstones and coffins with the ketchup and mustard.

6. Spread the lettuce on a platter with a high lip. Lean the gravestones against the lip to stand up. Nestle the coffins in the lettuce.

6. Delicious Grilled Two-Cheese Burgers with Garlic Dressing

Ingredients

For the sauce:
- 1/2 cup mayonnaise
- 3 tablespoons sour cream
- 3 tablespoons roughly chopped fresh basil (or chives, parsley, mint)
- 1 scallion (white and green parts), trimmed and roughly chopped
- 1 garlic clove, quartered
- 1/2 teaspoon Worcestershire sauce
- 1/4 teaspoon kosher salt
- 1/4 teaspoon ground black pepper

For the burgers:
- 1 1/4 pounds 80% lean ground beef
- 1 tablespoon vegetable oil
- 3/4 teaspoon kosher salt
- 1/2 teaspoon ground black pepper
- 1/4 cup shredded mozzarella cheese
- 4 hamburger buns
- 1 tomato, cored, thinly sliced, and lightly salted
- 2 tablespoons grated Parmesan cheese

Method

1. To make the sauce: Place the mayonnaise, sour cream, basil, scallion, garlic, Worcestershire sauce, salt, and pepper in the bowl of a food processor and puree until creamy and pale green. Transfer to a small bowl, cover with plastic wrap, and refrigerate until you are ready to use it.
2. To make the burgers: Heat a charcoal or gas grill to medium-high. Divide the ground beef into 4 equal pieces and gently form into patties. Use your thumb to make a small indentation in the middle of each burger (this is so the burger grills flat and doesn't contract and puff up on the grill). Brush both sides of the burgers with the oil and then season with salt and pepper.
3. Place the burgers on the grill and cook until they have grill marks, about 4 minutes. Flip the burgers, cook 2 minutes longer, and then top each with about 1 tablespoon of the mozzarella. Cook the burgers 2 more minutes for medium-rare doneness and remove from the grill. Place the buns on the grill, cut side down, and lightly toast, 30 seconds to 1 minute.
4. Set a burger on each bottom bun half. Top with a salted tomato slice. Spread 1 tablespoon of the garlic-herb sauce on the top bun half, sprinkle with Parmesan, cover the burger, and serve with more sauce on the side for dipping.

7. Amazing Adriatic

Ingredients

- 2 teaspoons extra virgin olive oil
- 32 heirloom red and yellow mixed grape tomatoes, halved lengthwise
- 4 tablespoons (2 ounces) unsalted butter, softened
- 1/4-1/2 teaspoon crushed red pepper flakes, to taste
- 1 clove garlic, halved
- 8 slices ciabatta or crusty bread
- 8 1/8-inch-thick slices Wisconsin Fresh Mozzarella cheese
- 2/3 cup (4 ounces) Wisconsin Feta cheese, crumbled
- 1 small red onion, thinly sliced
- 12 large basil leaves, roughly torn and a few sprigs for garnish
- 3 tablespoons balsamic glaze

Method

1. Heat oil in large nonstick skillet over medium-high heat. Add tomatoes, cut-side-down. Cook until starting to brown. Turn; cook until caramelized.

2. Combine butter and red pepper flakes. Rub 1 side of each bread slice with cut side of garlic. Spread same side with butter mixture. Place 4 slices, buttered-side-down, in skillet over medium heat.
3. Top each with 1 slice Mozzarella, tomatoes, Feta, onions, and basil; drizzle with balsamic glaze. Top with another Mozzarella slice and bread slice, buttered-side-up. Grill, turning once until bread is golden brown and cheese is melted. Garnish with basil sprigs, if desired.

8. Healthy Alpine

Ingredients

- Large handful stemmed kale, chopped
- 1 clove garlic, minced
- 1 tablespoon olive oil, divided
- Salt and freshly ground pepper
- 6-8 baby bella mushrooms, stems removed
- 1 teaspoon fresh rosemary, minced
- 3 tablespoons dry white wine
- 1-2 tablespoons butter, softened
- 4 slices sourdough bread
- 4 slices Wisconsin Alpine-style cheese
- 4 slices Wisconsin aged Swiss cheese

Method

1. Preheat oven to 350°F.
2. Make kale chips: Place kale and minced garlic in large mixing bowl. Drizzle with 1/2 tablespoon olive oil and season with pinch of salt and a few cracks of freshly ground pepper. Massage kale leaves with your hands to rub garlic into leaves and disperse olive oil and seasoning evenly (Using your hands is essential. A spoon or spatula will not penetrate and would require additional olive oil to coat evenly, risking soggy chips).

3. Spread kale on Silpat® or parchment paper-lined baking sheet, lying flat so leaves are not overlapping. Bake 12-15 minutes or until edges are dark brown; do not burn. Remove baking sheet from the oven to cool.

4. Meanwhile, slice baby bella mushroom caps and mince the fresh rosemary. Heat remaining 1/2 tablespoon olive oil in small saucepan over medium-high heat and add mushrooms, seasoning with a pinch of salt and a few cracks of freshly ground pepper; sauté 4 minutes while stirring. Reduce heat to medium and add the white wine and rosemary and cook an additional 4-5 minutes until wine has been absorbed and evaporated. Remove from heat and set aside.

5. Butter 1 side of each bread slice. Heat large skillet over medium heat and place the slices buttered-side-down in pan. Cover 2 slices of bread with 2 slices each of alpine-style cheese and cover remaining 2 slices of bread with swiss cheese. Place half the sautéed mushrooms over each Swiss cheese-covered slice, spreading evenly. Layer kale chips over mushrooms. Grill 4-5 minutes until the alpine-style cheese is melted. Using spatula, carefully flip alpine-topped slices onto the other 2 slices and press down to meld. Remove the grilled cheese from the skillet. Slice sandwiches in half if desired and serve immediately.

9. Healthy Amelia

Ingredients

- 1/8 cup sour cherries
- 1/8 cup blueberries
- 1/8 cup raspberries
- 4 tablespoons sugar, divided
- 1 tablespoon lemon juice
- 1/4 cup water
- 2 eggs
- 1/2 cup milk
- 2 teaspoons vanilla extract
- 1 pretzel baguette
- Butter for cooking
- 3 tablespoons Wisconsin Mascarpone cheese
- 1 tablespoon Wisconsin Brie cheese
- 1 tablespoon pistachios, crushed
- 2 ounces sliced prosciutto
- Powdered sugar for garnish

Method

1. For berry compote: Mix cherries, blueberries, raspberries, 2 tablespoons sugar, lemon juice and

water in pan. Simmer about 15 minutes over medium-low heat. Set aside to cool.

2. For French toast: Beat eggs, milk, remaining 2 tablespoons sugar and vanilla extract in shallow bowl. Cut pretzel bread into 4-inch-long pieces. Split the pieces for sandwiches. Then thinly slice off the tops and bottoms of bread to expose white of bread so it can absorb the batter better. Dip the bread pieces into the egg mixture, allowing each side to soak 1 minute. Melt butter in skillet over medium-low heat. Grill each side 2-3 minutes to brown. Avoid overcooking bread.

3. For cheese spread: Vigorously mix mascarpone, brie and pistachios with fork until well blended. Spread on inside of French toast slice, and allow bread to cool to room temperature. Drain any excess water and spread some of the fruit compote on top of the cheeses. Top with prosciutto slices and another slice of French toast. Sprinkle powdered sugar over.

10. Wonderful Athena

Ingredients

- 1 cucumber, peeled and seeded
- 2 cloves garlic, minced, divided
- 2 cups Greek yogurt, preferably whole milk
- 1 tablespoon honey
- Pinch of cayenne pepper
- Salt and pepper
- 2 cups kalamata olives, drained
- 1 tablespoon capers, rinsed
- 1-2 tablespoons flat-leaf (Italian) parsley leaves, rinsed and well dried
- 1 anchovy fillet
- 10 tablespoons extra virgin olive oil, divided
- 1-2 large eggplants
- 4 pieces flatbread
- 1 cup (6-8 ounces) Wisconsin Feta cheese, crumbled
- 1-2 heirloom or beefsteak tomatoes, sliced
- 1 red onion, thinly sliced

Method

1. Make tzatziki sauce: Grate cucumber on large holes of box grater; place in bowl. Add 1 clove minced garlic, Greek yogurt, honey, cayenne, and a pinch of salt. Mix well and refrigerate until serving time.
2. Make olive tapenade: Process olives, capers, parsley, remaining clove minced garlic, and anchovy fillet in food processor bowl with 4 tablespoons olive oil; process until smooth. Refrigerate until needed.
3. Slice eggplant(s) into 1/4- to 1/2-inch slices. Drizzle with olive oil and season with salt and pepper. Heat outdoor grill or stovetop griddle and grill eggplant slices for about 2 minutes a side. Set aside. Keep grill or griddle hot.
4. Cut flatbread pieces in half and place about 1 tablespoon of olive tapenade on each of 4 halves. Top with 1 ounce Feta, some tomato slices, onion slices, eggplant slices, another ounce of Feta, and flatbread half. Drizzle sandwich tops with a little olive oil and place, oil-side down, on hot grill. Grill about 3 minutes, then drizzle with a little more olive oil and flip. Grill until flatbread browns and cheese is heated through. Serve with tzatziki sauce on the side.

11. Delicious Bacon Habanero

Ingredients

- 6 slices bacon
- 2 tablespoons brown sugar
- 1 tablespoon butter
- 1 large Portobello mushroom, sliced thin
- 1 1/2 tablespoons balsamic glaze
- Salt and pepper
- 6 slices Wisconsin Habanero Jack cheese (about 2-3 ounces total)
- 2 slices pretzel bread
- Olive oil for drizzling

Method

1. Preheat oven to 375°F (400°F if bacon is thick sliced). Line jelly roll pan with foil. Place bacon strips, one by one, on foil. Sprinkle brown sugar over bacon. Bake until crisp, 15-20 minutes, depending on slice thickness. Remove from oven and drain on paper towels.
2. Heat butter in small skillet; add mushroom slices and cook about 5 minutes. Add balsamic glaze and season with salt and pepper. Preheat Panini press. Place bacon on bottom slice of bread. Layer slices of

Habanero Jack on top. Top with mushrooms and second piece of bread. Drizzle with olive oil and grill in Panini press about 8-10 minutes until golden and crunchy

12. Amazing Benedict

Ingredients

- 3 tablespoons white wine vinegar
- 4 eggs
- Salt and pepper
- 8 slices Canadian bacon
- 4 tablespoons butter, divided
- 4 English muffins, split
- 4 tablespoons Wisconsin Sharp Cheddar Cheese Spread, at room temperature
- 4 slices Wisconsin Gouda cheese
- 4 ounces fresh spinach leaves
- 1 tomato, sliced

Method

1. Heat 3-4 quarts water to just below boiling point. Add vinegar and pinch of salt. Gently stir the water. Lower heat so water is simmering. Crack eggs into the water one at a time and poach gently for 4-5 minutes. Remove with slotted spoon and season with salt and pepper.
2. Meanwhile, heat griddle or skillet over medium heat; fry Canadian bacon until lightly browned. Remove from griddle; set bacon aside. Add 1 tablespoon butter

to skillet. Spread each bottom half of English muffins with 1 tablespoon Sharp Cheddar cheese spread. Place in heated skillet. Top each bottom in pan with 1 slice Gouda, about 1 ounce spinach, 2 slices Canadian bacon, and 1 slice tomato. Cook over medium heat until cheese is melted. Remove to a plate and top each with a poached egg. Serve open-faced with remaining muffin halves, toasted and buttered, on the side.

13. Amazing Tex

Ingredients

- 1/4 teaspoon chili powder
- 1/8 teaspoon garlic powder
- 4 tablespoons butter, softened
- 4 slices hearty sourdough bread
- 4 slices Wisconsin Cheddar cheese
- 1 1/4 cups purchased or homemade macaroni and cheese, heated
- 4 slices fully cooked bacon, heated until crisp
- 4 slices Wisconsin Pepper Jack cheese
- 3/4 cup prepared chopped smoked beef brisket, heated
- 2 tablespoons honey smoked barbeque sauce (omit if brisket has sauce)
- 4 slices avocado
- 1 tablespoon pickled jalapeño chilies, finely chopped

Method

1. Mix chili powder and garlic powder into butter and spread on 1 side of 2 slices of bread, place buttered-side-down in large skillet over medium heat. Place 2 slices cheddar on each. Divide hot mac and

cheese evenly over each piece and top with another slice of bread. Butter tops and turn the sandwiches over. Top each sandwich with 2 pieces of bacon and 2 slices of pepper jack cheese.

2. Place hot brisket on top of one of the sandwiches; use slotted spoon to avoid excess liquid. Top with avocado and jalapeño. Carefully place the other sandwich cheese-side-down on top. Both sides should be golden brown. Cut in half and serve.

14. Amazing Buffalo Bill

Ingredients

- 4 boneless chicken breasts
- Salt and pepper
- 1 cup buttermilk
- 1 cup flour
- 1 cup spicy "buffalo wing" sauce
- Vegetable oil for frying
- 8 slices sourdough bread
- 6 tablespoons butter, at room temperature
- 4 slices Wisconsin Monterey Jack cheese
- 2/3 cup (4 ounces) Wisconsin Blue cheese, crumbled
- 2 cups iceberg lettuce, shredded
- Sweet pepper bruschetta topping, optional
- Hot sport peppers, optional

Method

1. Season chicken breasts with salt and pepper and place in zip-style resealable bag. Pour buttermilk into bag and seal. Refrigerate at least 1 hour or overnight.
2. Place flour on plate and season with salt and pepper. Pour wing sauce into bowl. Heat large sauté pan over medium-high heat. Add vegetable oil to about

1-inch depth and heat to 350°F. Remove chicken breasts from bag and roll in flour to coat. Fry in hot oil, 4-5 minutes per side, until golden and cooked through.

3. Remove chicken breasts from skillet with tongs and turn them in the bowl of hot sauce to coat evenly. Reserve on plate.

4. Heat large skillet over medium heat. Butter one side of each bread slice. Place 4 slices, butter-side down, in skillet and top each with 1 slice Monterey Jack, 1 chicken breast, 1 ounce Blue cheese crumbles, and 1/2 cup of shredded lettuce. Layer the sweet pepper bruschetta topping on the lettuce, if using. Top each sandwich with another piece of the bread, butter-side up, and grill, turning once, until bread is golden and cheese melts. Garnish with sport peppers, if desired.

15. Delicious Charlotte

Ingredients

- 1/2 cup balsamic vinegar
- 3 tablespoons honey
- 2 tablespoons olive oil, divided
- 1 cup red onion slices
- 1/4 pound Brussels sprouts, stemmed and quartered
- 3 large garlic cloves, minced
- 1/4 teaspoon salt
- 1/4 teaspoon pepper
- 1/2 teaspoon dried rosemary, crushed
- 1/2 teaspoon red pepper flakes
- 1/3 pound kielbasa sausage, sliced
- 1 tablespoon butter
- 4 thick slices rye bread
- 1 cup (about 3 ounces) Wisconsin Parmesan cheese, grated
- 6 1-ounce slices Wisconsin Havarti cheese

Method

1. Mix balsamic vinegar and honey in small saucepan and place over high heat. Bring to boil, reduce heat to low and simmer until mixture has

reduced to 1/4 cup, about 10 minutes. Set aside to cool.

2. Heat 1 tablespoon olive oil over medium-high in medium skillet. Add red onion slices; sauté until tender. Add remaining tablespoon olive oil, Brussels sprouts and garlic. Season with salt, pepper, rosemary and red pepper flakes. Sauté mixture until sprouts are browned and onions darken. Remove mixture to bowl and set aside.

3. In skillet onion mixture was cooked in, sear sausage over medium-high until browned. Remove from skillet and set aside. In same skillet, lower cooking temperature to medium and melt butter. Place 1 slice of bread in skillet. Top with half the parmesan, kielbasa sausage and onion and Brussels sprouts mixture. Drizzle some balsamic reduction over top. Layer 3 havarti cheese slices over and top with second slice of bread. Cover skillet and grill until first side is golden brown. Carefully flip sandwich and grill until golden brown. Remove sandwich and repeat steps for second sandwich. Halve sandwiches and serve.

16. Wonderful Delilah

Ingredients

- 5 strawberries, halved
- 1 teaspoon balsamic vinegar
- 1/8 teaspoon black pepper, freshly ground
- 4 slices country French bread
- 12 slices Wisconsin Brie cheese, rind removed
- 1/3 cup candied pecans, chopped
- 8 leaves fresh basil
- 4 slices prosciutto
- 2 tablespoons (1 ounce) butter

Method

1. Toss strawberries in balsamic vinegar and black pepper and set aside. Preheat skillet over medium heat. Lightly toast bread slices on 1 side and remove from skillet. Top toasted side of each slice with 3 slices of Brie and 1/4 of the candied pecans.
2. Top 2 of these slices with basil, strawberries and prosciutto. Cover with remaining 2 bread slices, untoasted-side-up. Melt half the butter in skillet over medium heat.

3.   Place sandwiches in skillet and butter tops with remaining butter. Grill sandwiches, flipping, until Brie has melted and bread is golden brown

17. Rhubarb and Baked Avocado

Ingredients

RHUBARB KETCHUP:
- 1 14.5-ounce can crushed tomatoes
- 1/4 teaspoon nutmeg
- 1 teaspoon maple syrup
- 1/2 teaspoon onion powder
- 1/2 teaspoon garlic powder
- 1/2 teaspoon chili powder
- 1/4 teaspoon chipotle chili powder
- 1/4 tablespoon sugar
- Salt and pepper, to taste
- 1 cup onion, diced
- 2/3 cup cider vinegar
- 4-5 stalks fresh rhubarb, cut in 1-inch pieces
- Hot sauce, to taste

FOR BAKED AVOCADOS:
- 1 cup panko breadcrumbs
- 1/2 teaspoon onion powder
- 1/2 teaspoon chili powder
- 1/2 cup flour
- Salt and pepper, to taste

- 1 egg
- 1 avocado, halved and pitted

FOR SANDWICH:
- 6 tablespoons butter, divided
- 2 eggs
- 4 slices French bread
- 4-6 slices Wisconsin Swiss cheese, divided
- Handful of watercress or other spicy green

Method

1. For ketchup: Place tomatoes in large saucepan. Add nutmeg, maple syrup, onion powder, garlic powder, chili powder, chipotle chili powder, sugar and generous pinch of salt and pepper. Add onions, vinegar and rhubarb; bring to boil over medium-high heat.

2. Add hot sauce to taste. Reduce heat; simmer, stirring frequently, 25-30 minutes, or until rhubarb is tender. Taste for seasoning after 20 minutes, adding additional salt or hot sauce to taste. Remove from heat and cool. Place ketchup in blender; blend until smooth. Set aside.

3. For avocados: Heat oven to 450°F. Line baking sheet or wire rack with foil. Place in oven. Mix breadcrumbs, onion powder, chili powder, salt and pepper in small bowl. Place flour in shallow second bowl. Crack egg into third bowl; beat gently. Cut each avocado half lengthwise into 3-4 slices.

4. Dredge avocado slice in flour, dip into egg to coat, then generously coat with breadcrumb mixture. Repeat with remaining avocado slices; place on hot foil-lined baking sheet or rack. Bake about 25 minutes, flipping halfway through. The breadcrumbs should be toasty brown but not burnt. Set aside.

5. To assemble sandwich: Heat 3 tablespoons butter in frying pan; fry egg sunny-side-up to desired doneness. Spread remaining butter on 1 side of each bread slice. Top unbuttered side of 2 bread slices with 1 or 2 Swiss cheese slices; place egg over cheese. Drizzle rhubarb ketchup over eggs.

6. Place half the avocado slices, watercress and remaining slices of Swiss on 2 remaining bread slices, unbuttered side. Heat grill or skillet over medium-high. Add sandwiches to pan and grill until toasty on both sides. Add a few additional sprigs of watercress to sandwiches and serve with additional ketchup. Unused ketchup may be stored, covered and refrigerated for 2 weeks.

18. Grilled Cheese Sandwich

Ingredients

- Method4 slices white bread
- 3 tablespoons butter, divided
- 2 slices Cheddar cheese

Method

1. Preheat skillet over medium heat. Generously butter one side of a slice of bread. Place bread butter-side-down onto skillet bottom and add 1 slice of cheese.
2. Butter a second slice of bread on one side and place butter-side-up on top of sandwich. Grill until lightly browned and flip over; continue grilling until cheese is melted. Repeat with remaining 2 slices of bread, butter and slice of cheese.

19. Delicious Pico De Gallo Grilled Cheese Sandwich

Ingredients

Pico de Gallo:
- 1 tomato, diced
- 1/2 white onion, diced
- 2 tablespoons chopped fresh cilantro, or to taste (optional)
- 1/2 lime, juiced salt and ground black pepper to taste

Sandwich:
- 3 tablespoons softened butter, or as needed
- 10 slices white bread
- 10 slices provolone cheese

Method

1. Mix tomato, onion, cilantro, lime juice, salt, and pepper together in a bowl.
2. Spread butter onto 1 side of each bread slice. Arrange bread, butter-side down, onto a work surface. Place 1 slice provolone cheese onto each bread slice and spoon pico de Gallo onto 5 of the bread-cheese

slices. Top each pico de Gallo layer with remaining bread-cheese slices, butter-side up.

3. Heat a skillet over medium heat. Grill each sandwich in the hot skillet until golden brown and cheese is melted, 3 to 4 minutes per side.

20. Delicious Grilled Cheese De Mayo

Ingredients

- 1 tablespoon mayonnaise, divided
- 2 slices white bread
- 2 slices American cheese
- 1 slice pepper jack cheese

Method

1. Spread 1/2 the mayonnaise onto one side of a slice of bread and place, mayonnaise-side down, in a skillet. Place American cheese and pepper jack cheese on top of the bread. Spread remaining mayonnaise onto one side of the remaining bread and place, mayonnaise-side up, on top of the cheese.
2. Cook sandwich in the skillet over medium heat until cheese melts and the bread is golden brown, about 2 1/2 minutes per side.

21. Tasty Grilled Cheese Sandwich

Ingredients

- 2 slices bacon
- 1 tablespoon smooth peanut butter
- 2 slices soft white bread
- 1 slice American cheese
- 1 tablespoon butter, softened

Method

1. Place the bacon in a large, deep skillet, and cook over medium-high heat, turning occasionally, until evenly browned, about 10 minutes. Drain the bacon slices on a paper towel-lined plate.
2. Spread peanut butter on a slice of white bread, and cover with cheese slice and bacon. Top with the other piece of bread. Spread butter on both sides of the sandwich, and pan-fry in a skillet over medium heat until the bread is golden brown and the cheese has melted, 2 to 3 minutes per side. Serve hot.

22. Delicious Grilled Cheese, Cinnamon, and Apple Sandwich

Ingredients

- 1 tablespoon softened butter
- 2 slices white bread
- 1 small apple - peeled, cored, and sliced
- 1/2 teaspoon ground cinnamon
- 1 slice American cheese

Method

1. Place a skillet over medium heat. Spread butter evenly and completely over one side of each bread slice. Arrange the apple slices on the unbuttered side of one of the bread slices.
2. Sprinkle the cinnamon over the apples. Place the cheese slice atop the apples. Top with the remaining bread slice with the buttered side facing outward. Lie gently into the skillet. Cook sandwich on both sides until golden brown, 2 to 3 minutes per side.

23. Tasty Bacon, Avocado, and Pepper jack Grilled Cheese Sandwich

Ingredients

- 8 (3/4 inch thick) slices sourdough bread
- 1/4 cup butter
- 8 slices cooked thick bacon
- 8 slices pepper jack cheese
- 1 red onion, sliced and separated into rings
- 1 avocado, halved and cut into 1/4-inch slices

Method

1. Lay bread on a work surface and spread butter on one side of each slice.
2. Layer bacon, 1 slice of cheese, onion rings, avocado slices, and another slice of cheese on top of the unbuttered-side of the bread; top with second slice of bread, buttered-side facing up.
3. Cook sandwiches in a skillet over medium heat, flipping once, until both sides are golden brown and cheese has melted, about 3 to 5 minutes per side.

24. Delicious Grilled Cheese with Gouda, Roasted Mushrooms and Onions

Ingredients

- 8 ounces mushrooms, sliced
- 1 medium onion, sliced (the sweeter the better)
- 2 tablespoons olive oil
- salt and pepper
- 4 tablespoons butter
- 4 slices bread of choice
- 1 cup gouda, shredded

Instructions

1. Preheat oven to 400°F.
2. On a baking sheet toss sliced mushrooms and onion in olive oil. Sprinkle with a few pinches of salt and pepper. Bake in oven for about 20 minutes, or until roasted to preference.
3. In a skillet stove top, melt 4 tablespoons butter over medium heat.
4. While butter is melting, assemble sandwiches. On one slice of bread, layer shredded gouda, the

roasted mushrooms and onions, then more gouda. (Layering this way ensures that the melty cheese will hold the sandwich together.) Salt and pepper to taste. Top with the other slice of bread. Lightly press together.

5. In the melted butter place one sandwich down for one second, then gently flip it over to the other side. Repeat with other sandwich. Cook for about 2 minutes, until lightly browned, then gently flip sandwich on other side, and cook for an additional 2-3 minutes, or until cheese is melted and sandwich is browned to preference.

25. Amazing Mediterranean Grilled Cheese Sandwich

Ingredients

- 2 slices rustic white bread or sourdough bread
- 1 Tbsp extra virgin olive oil, divided
- 2 oz. Wisconsin Whole Milk Mozzarella cheese, shredded
- 1 oz. Wisconsin Feta cheese, crumbled
- 2 cups fresh spinach
- 4 Roma tomato slices
- 2 Tbsp diced black olives
- 1 Tbsp finely chopped red onion
- 2 tsp chopped fresh basil
- 1/4 tsp finely minced garlic (about 1/3 clove)
- Freshly ground black pepper

Method

1. Heat 1 tsp olive oil in a non-stick 10-inch skillet over medium-high heat. Once hot, add garlic and spinach and saute until spinach begins to wilt, about 30 seconds. Remove from heat, stir in basil and set aside.
2. To assemble sandwich, spread Mozzarella and Feta cheese over one slice of bread into an even layer.

Layer tomatoes in a single layer over cheese. Spread spinach mixture over tomatoes then sprinkle olives and red onions over tomatoes. Season with freshly ground black pepper and top with remaining slice of bread.

3. Spread 1 tsp olive oil evenly over skillet, add sandwich and heat over medium-low heat. Cook until bottom is golden brown, about 3 - 4 minutes, then remove sandwich from pan.

4. Spread remaining 1 tsp olive oil evenly along skillet, carefully rotate sandwich to opposite side and return to pan over medium-low heat. Cover skillet with lid and cook until bottom is golden brown, about 2 - 3 minutes. Serve immediately.

26. Amazing Green Goddess Grilled Cheese Sandwich

Ingredients

- 2 slices bread
- 2-3 tablespoons Green Goddess Herb Pesto
- 2 slices mild white melty cheese like mozzarella
- handful fresh baby spinach
- ¼ avocado, sliced
- 2 tablespoons goat cheese, crumbled
- olive oil (and butter if you're so inclined)

Method

1. Spread about 1 tablespoon of Green Goddess Herb Pesto onto each slice of bread (2 tablespoons total, but if you're sensitive, go light, the pesto is STRONG).
2. On one slice of bread, add 1 slice of cheese, sliced avocado, crumbled goat cheese, spinach, second slice of cheese, then top it with second slice of bread. Press together gently.
3. Heat 1 tablespoon olive oil in a frying pan over medium low heat. (If you want to use butter, add it to the oil and let it melt). Add the sandwich to the oil and

cook until bread is golden brown. Press down on the sandwich lightly, then flip the sandwich over and cook until second side is golden brown.

27. Healthy Balsamic Blueberry Grilled Cheese Sandwich

Ingredients

- 2 slices of bread (I used sourdough)
- Plenty of white cheese (I used Havarti, but lots of different cheeses would be good! Mozzarella, Monterey, Swiss, or Sharp White Cheddar would be yummy. I have been meaning to try goat cheese!)
- Fresh spinach or arugula
- 1/2 cups fresh or frozen blueberries
- 1 tbs balsamic vinegar
- 1 1/2 tbs. brown sugar

Method

1. In a small saucepan, combine blueberries, sugar and vinegar. Turn on medium heat and let come to a slow boil. Use a utensil to crush berries as you stir. After boiling for about 5 minutes, pour mixture into a mesh strainer and let the juice syrup separate from the solid berries. Save the syrup for cocktails, pancakes or both!
2. Spread blueberries onto a piece of bread, top with cheese, some spinach, then more cheese! Sprinkle

with fresh ground pepper. Top with your other slice of bread and toast. Enjoy!

28. Tasty Hawaiian Grilled Cheese

Ingredients

- 2 slices of bread
- 3 slices of pineapple, fresh or canned
- 3 slices Canadian bacon
- shredded Monterey Jack cheese
- butter
- oregano and parsley

Method

1. Butter one side of each slice of bread and sprinkle with parsley and oregano to taste
2. On non-buttered side of bread place the shredded cheese, then the canadian bacon, pineapple, and top with the other slice of bread, buttered side facing up.
3. Cook sandwich on stove top on a griddle or frying pan. Once bread is toasted on one side flip the sandwich to toast the other side. Cook on a low heat to allow the cheese to melt while the bread is toasting.

29. Healthy Grilled Cheese Rolls

Ingredients

- 6 slices wheat bread
- 6 pieces American cheese
- 1 tablespoon butter

Method

1. Cut the crusts off the bread.
2. Flatten your crust less bread squares with a rolling pin and then top each slice of bread with one piece of cheese (don't be tempted to use more cheese; in this case, one is plenty).
3. Melt butter in pan over medium heat.
4. Roll your cheese squares up and cook them in the melted butter over medium heat, seam-side down first to secure them, for about five minutes until cheese is melted. Roll them occasionally while cooking to crisp all sides.
5. Remove from the pan and your grilled cheese rolls are ready to enjoy!

30. Amazing Avocado-Green-Red-Grated Cheese-sliced Bread

Ingredients

- red onion, thinly sliced: ¼ cup
- lime juice: 2 teaspoons
- roasted red pepper, drained (if in a marinade) and finely chopped: ¼ cup
- mayonnaise: 1 teaspoon
- garlic, minced: ½ teaspoon
- salted butter: 2 tablespoons, divided
- whole wheat sandwich bread: 2 (½-inch) slices from a large loaf
- Manchego cheese, grated: 1 cup
- cured chorizo: 4 large, thin slices
- avocado: ¾ of a small to medium-sized avocado
- sea salt and freshly ground black pepper: to taste

Method

1. Add the red onions to a small bowl and drizzle with the lime juice. This will quickly pickle them. Set aside.

2. In another small bowl, combine the red pepper with the mayonnaise and garlic. Add a pinch of salt and pepper and set aside.
3. Preheat a heavy-bottomed skillet (preferably cast iron) over medium-high heat. Spread about 2 teaspoons of the butter on one side of each slice of bread. Then spread half of the pepper mixture on the other side of each slice.
4. Place both slices of bread, buttered side down, in the preheated skillet, and then distribute half of the cheese to each slice of bread, over the red pepper mixture. Reduce the heat to medium-low. Grated cheese-toast
5. Once the cheese is melting, add the chorizo slices on top of one of the slices of bread.
6. Peel the avocado, cut about ¾ of it into bite-sized pieces, and place them in a small bowl. Add the lime-pickled onions and gently mix the two together. Season with a pinch of salt and pepper.
7. Spoon the avocado-onion mixture over the chorizo slices.
8. Close the sandwich and gently press it down with a flat-bottomed spatula. Add 1 teaspoon of the remaining butter to the empty part of the pan and move the sandwich onto it. Let it cook for about a minute or so. Move it to the side, add the final teaspoon of butter to the pan, and carefully flip the sandwich over, onto the butter. Cook for another minute and remove from the pan. When it's done, both sides of the bread should be golden brown and

everything should be more or less held together with the melted cheese.

9. Remove the sandwich from the pan, cut it in half, and serve.

31. Healthy Beet, Arugula & Goat Cheese Grilled Cheese

Ingredients

- 1-2 Beets
- Olive Oil
- Arugula
- Goat Cheese
- Butter
- French Bread
- 1/2 ounce sherry (optional)
- Salt

Method

1. Start off by roasting the beets by your preferred method. I skinned them with a paring knife, sliced them evenly, tossed them in some olive oil and salt, then baked on 375°F for 20-30 minutes, flipping halfway through.

2.   Once the beets have cooked to your desired tenderness (poke them with a fork or taste a few slices), take them out of the oven and in a pan on medium-high heat, quickly fry them with about a ½ ounce of sherry wine, cooking until evaporated. After thinking about it, you could also try cooking them in some red/white wine or some balsamic vinegar, as I think they would add some nice flavors to the beets. (Next time I may try tossing the arugula in some balsamic vinegar, could be tasty!).

3.   Once you have finished frying the beets, slice up your bread, butter each side, lay down some arugula, a little bit of goat cheese, then your beets and some more goat cheese, and slap it together!

4.   Fry the sandwich in a pan on medium heat until each side is golden brown, then sliced it in half and enjoy!

32. Corned Beef with Mustard and Cheese

Ingredients

- honey: 1½ tablespoons
- whole grain mustard: 1½ tablespoons
- unsalted butter: 1 tablespoon
- your favorite bread: 2 thick slices
- gruyere cheese: just enough to cover both pieces of bread (¼ inch slices)
- corned beef (presumably left over): just enough to cover the cheese on one of the pieces of bread (¼ inch slices)
- sautéed, shredded cabbage (presumably left over): about ¼ cup

Method

1. In a small bowl, mix the honey with the mustard.
2. Spread an even layer of the honey mustard on one side of each slice of bread. Melt the butter in a medium sized sauté pan, over medium-low heat, and add both slices of bread, honey mustard–side up.
3. Add the slices of cheese, in one layer, to both slices of bread.

4. Place the corned beef slices, in one layer, on top of the cheese on one of the pieces of bread.
5. Add the cabbage on top of the corned beef.
6. Once the cheese has melted, add the other slice of bread to complete the sandwich. Use a flat-bottomed spatula to gently press down on the top to bring all of the ingredients together.
7. Remove from the pan and eat!

33. Delicious Roasted Tomato Soup with Grilled Cheese Croutons

Ingredients

- 6 cups (3 pints) cherry tomatoes
- 3 tablespoons olive oil
- 1 teaspoon salt
- 1/2 teaspoon pepper
- 2 tablespoons unsalted butter
- 2 garlic cloves, minced
- 1 cup chopped onion
- 1 (28-ounce) can diced tomatoes
- 4 cups chicken broth
- 1/2 teaspoon thyme
- 1 cup whipping cream

Method

1. Heat the oven to 400°. On a baking sheet, combine the cherry tomatoes, 2 tablespoons of the olive oil, and the salt and pepper. Toss the ingredients to coat evenly and spread them in a single layer. Roast the tomatoes until they are shriveled with brown spots, about 35 to 45 minutes.
2. In a large pot, heat the butter and the remaining tablespoon of oil over medium heat. Add the garlic and

onion and sauté until softened, about 6 minutes. Add the canned tomatoes with their juice, the broth, the thyme, and the roasted tomatoes, including any liquid on the baking sheet. Bring the mixture to a boil, then reduce the heat and simmer, partially covered, for 40 minutes.

3. Using a food processor or blender, puree the soup until it's smooth. Return it to the pot and stir in the cream. Without letting the soup boil, warm it over medium heat, stirring often, until steaming. Add salt and pepper, if necessary.

34. Delicious Grilled cheese croutons:

Ingredients

- 1/4 cup unsalted butter, softened
- 1/4 teaspoon thyme
- 6 thin slices of bread
- 3 ounces Cheddar, thinly sliced

1. Heat a large skillet over medium-high heat. In a small bowl, combine the butter and thyme. Spread one side of each bread slice with the butter mixture.
2. Place 3 slices in the pan, buttered side down. Top with the cheese, then with the remaining 3 bread slices, buttered side up.
3. Cook, turning once, until toasted on both sides, 3 to 5 minutes per side. Remove the sandwiches from the pan. Let them cool slightly, then cut them into 1-inch squares. Makes about 60 croutons.

35. Amazing Grilled Cheese with Gouda, Roasted Mushrooms and Onions

Ingredients

- 8 ounces mushrooms, sliced
- 1 medium onion, sliced (the sweeter the better)
- 2 tablespoons olive oil
- salt and pepper
- 4 tablespoons butter
- 4 slices bread of choice
- 1 cup gouda, shredded

Method

1. Preheat oven to 400°F.
2. On a baking sheet toss sliced mushrooms and onion in olive oil. Sprinkle with a few pinches of salt and pepper. Bake in oven for about 20 minutes, or until roasted to preference.
3. In a skillet stove top, melt 4 tablespoons butter over medium heat.
4. While butter is melting, assemble sandwiches. On one slice of bread, layer shredded Gouda, the

roasted mushrooms and onions, then more Gouda. (Layering this way ensures that the melty cheese will hold the sandwich together.) Salt and pepper to taste. Top with the other slice of bread. Lightly press together.

5.   In the melted butter place one sandwich down for one second, then gently flip it over to the other side. Repeat with other sandwich. Cook for about 2 minutes, until lightly browned, then gently flip sandwich on other side, and cook for an additional 2-3 minutes, or until cheese is melted and sandwich is browned to preference.

Part 2

Introduction

Grilling is one of the basic methods of cooking food. While barbecue is considered a form of art because of the variety of ingredients used and the kind of preparation is more complex.

Grilling or Barbecue is no longer just a summer activity where everyone is gathered for a barbecue party. At present, people around the world enjoy grilling food at any time of the year!

You too can indulge in the joy of grilling! Simply follow the recipes in this book, and you can never go wrong.

Here are some helpful tips on grilling:
- If you're using wooden skewers, soak them in water for 20 to 30 minutes before using them. This will prevent them from burning while on the grill.
- Cover exposed bones with aluminum foil so that they do not get burned in the process.
- Keep an instant-read thermometer nearby. It is a very handy tool that you can use to find out if your food is cooked already.
- Fruits and vegetables are just as yummy when they are grilled as meat are. Don't limit yourself to grilling meat!

- Remember to lightly oil the grill grate before use. This will help your food cook without sticking onto the grill.

This book provides you many grilled and barbecue recipes that you can use to include in planning meals for you and your family. It includes grilled meat, poultry, fish, seafood, vegetable, and even fruit recipes that you will surely enjoy.

This book is a part of many cookbook series that I am writing; I hope you have fun trying all the recipes in this book.

So now, let's get it started!

Chicken Satay with Spicy Peanut Sauce

The peanut sauce tastes extremely good and that it complements well with the chicken.

Preparation time: 2 hours 10 minutes
Total time: 2 hours 30 minutes
Yield: 8 servings

Ingredients
1 pound of chicken fillet, cut into 1-inch pieces (450 g)

Marinade:
1/2 cup of coconut milk (125 ml)
2 cloves of garlic, minced (6 g)
2 teaspoons of brown sugar (10 g)
1 teaspoon of curry powder (2 g)

1/2 teaspoon of salt (2.5 g)
1/2 teaspoon of pepper (1 g)

Satay Sauce:
1 cup of coconut milk (250 ml)
1 teaspoons of curry powder (2 g)
1/2 cup of peanut butter (125 g)
3/4 cup of chicken stock (185 ml)
1/4 cup of brown sugar (55 g)
2 tablespoons of lime juice (30 ml)
1 teaspoon of soy sauce (5 ml)
1 red hot chili pepper, chopped (2 g)
salt and freshly ground black pepper

Method

1. Combine the coconut milk with the garlic, curry powder, brown sugar, pepper, and salt. Stir until the sugar has dissolved then transfer the marinade to a non-reactive container with the chicken. Cover and marinate for 2 hours.

2. Preheat your grill to medium-high heat.

3. Thread your marinated chicken onto each skewer, about three or four pieces of chicken. Grill on each side for 5 minutes.

4. To make the spicy peanut sauce, simmer the 1 cup of coconut milk, peanut butter, chicken stock, curry powder, 1/4 cup of brown sugar, and chili in a saucepan over medium-high heat for 5 minutes,

stirring frequently. Remove from heat then stir in the lime juice and soy sauce. Season with salt and pepper to taste.

5. Serve chicken skewers in a serving platter with spicy peanut sauce on the side.

6. Enjoy.

Nutritional Information:

Energy - 268 calories
Fat - 20.6 g
Carbohydrates - 12.5 g
Protein - 11.6 g
Sodium - 358 mg

Chicken Shish Kabobs

The cherry tomatoes add a beautiful contrast to this savory dish.

Preparation Time: 2 hours 10 minutes
Total Time: 2 hours 30 minutes
Yield: 8 servings

Ingredients
1/4 cup of olive oil (60 ml)
1/4 cup of lemon juice (60 ml)
1 teaspoon of garlic, minced (3 g)
1 teaspoon of ground cumin (2 g)
1/2 teaspoon of dried oregano (1 g)
1/2 teaspoon of dried thyme (1 g)
1/4 teaspoon of salt
1/4 teaspoon of black pepper (ground)
2.2 pounds of chicken fillet, cut into 1 1/2-inch pieces (1 kg)

1 cup cherry tomatoes (150 g)
cooking oil spray
salt and freshly ground black pepper

Method
1. In a bowl, mix together the olive oil, lemon juice, garlic, cumin, dried oregano, and dried thyme. Add in the chicken and toss to coat. Season with salt and pepper to taste. Cover the bowl with some cling wrap and allow to marinate in the fridge for 2 hours.
2. Preheat your grill to medium-high heat and spray the grate with oil.
3. Thread pieces of chicken and cherry tomatoes onto each skewer. (You can choose to thread in the cherry tomatoes or to grill them separately)
4. Cook the skewered chicken on the grill. Turn frequently so it's evenly brown on all sides. This should take about 10-15 minutes.
5. Place the cooked skewers into a serving dish.
6. Serve and enjoy.

Nutritional Information:

Energy - 282 calories
Fat - 14.9 g
Carbohydrates - 2.3 g
Protein - 33.4 g

Sodium - 175 mg

Flame-Grilled Steak

If you are looking for a flavorful grilled steak, this is the perfect recipe for you!

Preparation time: 2 hours 10 minutes
Total time: 2 hours 30 minutes
Yield: 4 servings

Ingredients

1/4 cup of olive oil (60 ml)
2 tablespoons of soy sauce (30 ml)
1 tablespoon of Worcestershire sauce (15 ml)
1 teaspoon of garlic, minced (3 g)
1 medium onion, chopped (110 g)
1/4 teaspoon of dried rosemary
4 (6 oz.) beef sirloin steaks (700 g)
3 tablespoons of steak sauce (45 g)
salt and freshly ground black pepper

Method

1. Mix together in a non-reactive bowl the olive oil, soy sauce, Worcestershire sauce, garlic, onion, and dried rosemary. Add the steaks and turn to coat all sides. Cover and refrigerate for 2 hours
2. Preheat your grill to high.
3. Once ready, flame grill the steaks for about 5-7 minutes on each side (depends on your preferred doneness). Brushing with steak sauce frequently.
4. Transfer into a serving dish.
5. Enjoy.

Nutritional Information:
Energy - 330 calories
Fat - 17.6 g
Carbohydrates - 6.2 g
Protein - 35.0 g
Sodium - 553 mg

Flame-Grilled Beef Burgers

This creamy and spicy marinade recipe is bursting with wonderful flavors.

Preparation time: 15 minutes
Total Time: 25 minutes
Yield: 8 servings

Ingredients
2.2 pounds of ground beef (1 kg)
1 (1 oz.) package of ranch dressing mix (28 g)
1 large whole egg (60 g)
3/4 cup of saltine crackers (crushed)
1 medium chopped onion (110 g)
2 tablespoons fresh coriander (7 g)
fresh ground black pepper

Method
1. Preheat your grill to high.

2. Mix together the ground beef, ranch dressing mix, egg, saltine crackers, onion, and coriander in a bowl. Divide and form mixture into 8 burger patties.

3. Flame grill each patty for 5 minutes on each side.

4. Transfer into a serving dish.

5. Serve and enjoy.

Nutritional Information:

Energy - 243 calories
Fat - 8.1 g
Carbohydrates - 4.5 g
Protein - 35.6 g
Sodium - 145 mg

Grilled Chicken Drumstick with Rosemary

Chicken and rosemary are perfect together, serve this tonight for dinner!

Preparation time: 2 hours 10 minutes
Total time: 2 hours 30 minutes
Yield: 4 servings

Ingredients
3 tablespoons of olive oil (45 ml)
1 1/2 tablespoons of Dijon mustard (20 ml)
1 tablespoon fresh rosemary, chopped (3.5 g)
1 tablespoon of lemon juice (15 ml)
1/2 teaspoon garlic, minced (1.5 g)
4 chicken drumsticks (450 g)
salt and freshly ground black pepper
cooking oil spray

Method

1. Whisk together the olive oil, Dijon mustard, rosemary, lemon juice, and garlic in a non-reactive bowl.

2. Add the chicken and turn to coat all sides. Season with salt and pepper to taste. Cover and refrigerate for 2 hours.

3. Preheat your grill to medium-high. Spray the grate with oil.

4. Grill the chicken for 5-7 minutes and turn it over to grill on the other side.

5. Transfer cooked drumsticks into a serving dish.

6. Serve and enjoy.

Nutritional Information:

Energy - 254 calories
Fat - 16.1 g
Carbohydrates - 1.0 g
Protein - 25.7 g
Sodium - 141 mg

Grilled Cumin Lamb Chops

Delicious, juicy, and very simple to make.

Preparation Time: 2 hours 10 minutes
Total Time: 2 hours 30 minutes
Yield: 4 servings

Ingredients
1/4 cup of white vinegar (60 ml)
2 tablespoons of olive oil (30 ml)
1 teaspoon of minced garlic (3 g)
1/2 teaspoon of cumin (1 g)
1/2 medium onion, finely chopped (55 g)
4 lamb chops (450 g)
salt and freshly ground black pepper

Method

1. Take a resealable bag and mix the vinegar, olive oil, garlic, cumin, and onion in it. Season with salt and pepper to taste.
2. Add the lamb and massage it with the marinade. Marinate in the fridge for at least 2 hours.
3. Preheat your grill to medium-high.
4. Take the lamb out of the resealable bag. Wrap the bones of the lamb with some aluminum foil; this will keep them from burning.
5. Grill lamb chops for about 5 minutes on each side.
6. Transfer cooked lamb chops into a serving dish.
7. Serve and enjoy.

Nutritional Information:

Energy - 283 calories
Fat - 19.2 g
Carbohydrates - 1.8 g
Protein - 24.2 g
Sodium - 223 mg

Spiced Lamb Skewers

If big chunks of lamb aren't your cup of tea, these bite-sized pieces might be!

Preparation time: 2 hours 10 minutes
Total time: 2 hours 30 minutes
Yield: 8 servings

Ingredients
2.2 pounds of boneless lamb shoulder, cut into 1-inch pieces (1 kg)
1/2 cup of Greek yogurt (125 g)
2 tablespoons of Dijon mustard (30 g)
1/2 teaspoon of curry powder (1 g)
1/2 teaspoon of turmeric powder (1 g)
1/2 teaspoon of dried oregano (1 g)

2 cloves of garlic, chopped (6 g)
salt and freshly ground black pepper
8 metal skewers

Method

1. In a non-reactive bowl, mix together the yogurt, Dijon mustard, curry powder, turmeric, oregano, and garlic.
2. Add the beef and season with salt and pepper to taste. Marinate your lamb for at least 2 hours.
3. Preheat your grill to high.
4. Thread the lamb with a skewers.
5. Grill for about 5-7 minutes on each side or to your desired doneness.
6. Transfer cooked skewers into a serving dish.
7. Serve and enjoy.

Nutritional Information:

Energy - 212 calories
Fat - 14.2 g
Carbohydrates - 1.9 g
Protein - 25.2 g
Sodium - 183 mg

Grilled Lemon Butter Shrimp

A simple yet delicious dish that you can serve to any occasion.

Preparation time: 35 minutes
Total time: 50 minutes
Yield: 4 servings (2 skewers each)

Ingredients
1 pound shrimps, peeled with tails still on (450 g)
4 tablespoons of butter (60 g)
2 tablespoons of lemon juice (30 ml)
2 cloves of garlic, minced (6 g)
1/2 teaspoon of dried sage (1 g)
salt and freshly ground black pepper

8 wooden skewers

Method
1. In a medium bowl, combine butter, lemon juice, garlic, and sage.
2. Add the shrimps. Season with salt and pepper to taste. Let sit for 15 minutes.
3. Preheat your grill to high.
4. Divide and thread shrimps onto skewers.
5. Grill the shrimps until they become pink in color and grill marks are formed, about 3 minutes on each side.
6. Serve immediately and enjoy.

Nutritional Information:
Energy - 241 calories
Fat - 13.5 g
Carbohydrates - 2.4 g
Protein - 25.1 g
Sodium - 508 mg

Spicy Grilled Shrimp

Grilling shrimp with some spices enhances its flavor.

Preparation time: 10 minutes
Total time: 20 minutes
Yield: 4 servings

Ingredients
1/4 cup of olive oil (60 ml)
2 tablespoons of lemon juice (30 ml)
2 cloves of garlic, minced (6 g)
1/2 teaspoon of paprika (1 g)
1/2 teaspoon of cayenne pepper (1 g)
1 pound of large shrimps (450 g)
salt and freshly ground black pepper
cooking oil spray

Method

1. Preheat your grill or griddle to medium-high heat. Spray the grate with oil.
2. Mix together the olive oil, lemon juice, garlic, paprika, and cayenne pepper in a medium bowl.
3. Add the shrimps and toss to coat. Season with salt and pepper to taste.
4. Cook the shrimp for 3 minutes on each side or until just cooked.
5. Serve immediately and enjoy.

Nutritional Information:

Energy - 248 calories
Fat - 14.7 g
Carbohydrates - 2.7 g
Protein - 26.1 g
Sodium - 326 mg

Grilled Rack of Lamb with Mixed Herbs

This succulent grilled lamb recipe is perfect for weekend dinners.

Preparation time: 2 hours and 10 minutes
Total time: 2 hours 30 minutes
Yield: 8 servings

Ingredients
1/2 cup of olive oil (125 ml)
1/4 cup of lemon juice (60 ml)
2 tablespoons of fresh cilantro, chopped (7 g)
2 tablespoons of fresh parsley, chopped (7 g)
2 tablespoons of fresh mint, chopped (7 g)
2 tablespoons of rosemary, chopped (7 g)
4 cloves of garlic, minced (12 g)
2 racks of lamb (1 ½ lbs. or 700 g each)
salt and freshly ground black pepper

cooking oil spray

Method
1. In a small bowl, mix together olive oil, lemon juice, cilantro, parsley, mint, and garlic. Season with salt and pepper to taste.
2. Take a spoon and spread this mixture over the 2 racks of lamb.
3. Wrap the exposed bones with foil to keep them from burning.
4. Preheat your grill to high. Spray grate with oil.
5. Grill the racks for about 7-8 minutes per side or to your desired doneness. Baste with remaining herb mixture. Remove from grill and let it rest for a few minutes before slicing.
6. Serve and enjoy.

Nutritional Information:

Energy - 273 calories
Fat - 14.8 g
Carbohydrates - 1.4 g
Protein - 32.1 g
Sodium - 89 mg

Grilled Scallops with Garlic and Scallions

The addition of garlic and scallions enhance the taste of this wonderful scallop dish.

Preparation time: 10 minutes
Total time: 20 minutes
Yield: 8 servings

Ingredients

1/2 cup of unsalted butter, melted (120 g)
1/4 cup of lemon juice (60 ml)
4 cloves of garlic, chopped (12 g)
1 1/2 pounds of scallops, prepared and half-shelled (700 g)
1/4 cup of scallions, chopped (30 g)
salt and freshly ground black pepper
cooking oil spray

Method

1. Preheat your outdoor grill to high. Spray the grate with oil.
2. Combine butter, lemon juice, and garlic in a small bowl. Season with salt and pepper to taste. Spoon mixture over each scallop. Sprinkle with chopped scallions.
3. Grill the scallops until opaque and just cooked.
4. Transfer cooked scallops into a serving platter.
5. Serve and enjoy.

Nutritional Information:
Energy - 173 calories
Fat - 8.6 g
Carbohydrates - 3.6 g
Protein - 19.3 g
Sodium - 239 mg"

Grilled Seafood on Skewers

You can go wild with the seafood combinations. They

all taste good together.

Preparation time: 15 minutes
Total time: 55 minutes
Yield: 8 servings (2 skewers each)

Ingredients
1 pound of seafood mix - squid, shrimp, scallop, mussel, salmon, etc., (450 g)
1/4 cup of soy sauce (60 ml)
1/4 cup of honey (80 ml)
1 tablespoon of rice vinegar (15 ml)
1 teaspoon of fresh ginger root, minced (5 g)
1 clove of garlic, minced (3 g)
salt and freshly ground black pepper

cooking oil spray
8 wooden skewers

Method
1. Cut your seafood into small pieces.
2. Combine the soy sauce, honey, vinegar, ginger, and garlic in a non-reactive bowl. Add the seafood mix. Let sit for 30 minutes.
3. Thread seafood onto each skewer. Reserve marinade and cook over medium heat for 5-7 minutes.
4. Preheat your grill or griddle to medium-high heat. Spray grate with oil.
5. Cook the seafood for 3-4 minutes on each side, brushing them with the marinade frequently.
6. Transfer into a serving dish.
7. Serve and enjoy.

Nutritional Information:
Energy - 173 calories
Fat - 1.4 g
Carbohydrates - 12.2 g
Protein - 27.1 g
Sodium - 590 mg

Grilled Trout with Onion and Herbs

Very easy to cook and oh so yummy!

Preparation time: 15 minutes
Total time: 30 minutes
Yield: 8 servings

Ingredients
2 (1 lb. or 450 g) whole trout
1/4 cup of olive oil, divided (60 ml)
1/2 medium lemon, juiced and zested (50 g)
2 cloves of garlic (6 g)
2 sprigs of rosemary, chopped (2 g)
2 sprigs of thyme, chopped (2 g)
1 large white onion, thinly sliced (150 g)
salt and freshly ground black pepper

Method
1. Preheat your grill to high.

2. Combine olive oil, lemon juice, zest, garlic, rosemary, and thyme in a small bowl. Season with salt and pepper to taste. Mix well. Rub mixture onto each trout including the crevices.
3. Place each trout in a fish basket and top with onion slices.
4. Grill fish for 7-10 minutes on each side, flipping once or until cooked through.
5. Transfer into a serving dish.
6. Serve and enjoy.

Nutritional Information:

Energy - 224 calories
Fat - 12.4 g
Carbohydrates - 2.8 g
Protein - 24.4 g
Sodium - 149 mg

Grilled Tuna Belly with Dill

If you are staying away from grilled meat, this grilled tuna belly with dill is perfect for you.

Preparation time: 10 minutes
Total time: 1 hour 20 minutes
Yield: 4 servings

Ingredients
4 (6 oz. or 180 g) tuna steaks
¼ cup of extra virgin olive oil (60 ml)
2 tablespoons lemon juice (30 ml)
1 tablespoon honey (20 ml)
2 tablespoons fresh dill weed, chopped (7 g)
salt and freshly ground black pepper
cooking oil spray

Method
1. Combine olive oil, lemon juice, honey, and dill weed in a resealable plastic bag.

2. Add the tuna steaks. Season with salt and pepper to taste. Seal and shake a bit to coat all sides of the fish. Refrigerate for at least an hour.

3. Preheat the grill to high. Spray grate with oil.

4. Cook the tuna steaks on the grill for 5-7 minutes on each side.

5. Transfer into a serving platter. Garnish with some fresh dill weed, if desired.

6. Serve and enjoy.

Nutritional Information:

Energy - 283 calories
Fat - 19.2 g
Carbohydrates - 1.8 g
Protein - 24.2 g
Sodium - 223 mg

Peanut Marinated Chicken Satay

Great for parties or weekend dinners. These chicken

skewers is a sure hit!

Preparation time: 2 hours 10 minutes
Total Time: 2 hours 30 minutes
Yield: 6 servings (2 skewers each)

Ingredients
2 tablespoons peanut oil (30 ml)
2 tablespoons of peanut butter (40 g)
2 tablespoons of soy sauce (30 ml)
2 tablespoons of lemon juice (30 ml)
1 tablespoon of brown sugar (15 g)
2 teaspoons of curry powder (4 g)
2 cloves of garlic, crushed (6 g)
1 teaspoon of hot sauce (5 ml)
1 ½ pounds chicken breast fillet, diced (700 g)

salt and freshly ground black pepper
12 wooden skewers

Method
1. Combine the peanut oil, peanut butter, soy sauce, lemon juice, brown sugar, curry powder, garlic, and hot sauce in a non-reactive bowl.
2. Add the chicken into the marinade. Season with salt and pepper to taste. Cover and refrigerate for at least 2 hours.
3. Preheat your grill to high.
4. Thread the chicken onto each skewer.
5. Grill the skewers for 5-7 minutes on each side or until cooked through.
6. Transfer into a serving platter.
7. Serve and enjoy.

Nutritional Information:

Energy - 279 calories
Fat - 13.9 g
Carbohydrates - 2.8 g
Protein - 34.2 g
Sodium - 359 mg

Grilled Steak with Homemade Balsamic Marinade

A grilled steak recipe marinated in sweet and tangy marinade made with olive oil, balsamic vinegar, honey, and fresh herbs.

Preparation time: 2 hours 10 minutes
Total time: 2 hours 30 minutes
Yield: 4 servings

Ingredients
4 (6 oz. or 180 g) sirloin steaks
2/3 cup of olive oil (170 ml)
1/3 cup of balsamic vinegar (85 ml)
3 cloves of garlic, minced (9 g)

1 tablespoon of honey (20 ml)
1 tablespoon fresh rosemary, chopped (3.5 g)
1 teaspoon of paprika (2 g)
salt and freshly ground black pepper
red peppercorns

Method

1. To make the marinade, combine the olive oil, balsamic vinegar, garlic, honey, rosemary, and paprika in a small bowl. Season with salt and pepper, to taste.
2. Place the steaks in a non-reactive container with lid and pour the marinade over them. Turn to coat all sides of the steaks. Cover with a lid and refrigerate for at least 2 hours.
3. Preheat your grill to high.
4. Grill each side of the steaks for 5-7 minutes on each side or to your desired doneness. Sprinkle with some red peppercorns on top of the steaks before serving, for added flavor.
5. Transfer into a serving dish.
6. Serve and enjoy.

Nutritional Information:

Energy - 309 calories

Fat - 15.4 g
Carbohydrates - 6.1 g
Protein - 34.7 g
Sodium - 224 mg

Grilled Beef Skewers with Indian Spice Marinade

This Indian-inspired beef skewer recipe is so delicious!

Preparation time: 2 hours 10 minutes
Total time: 2 hours 30 minutes
Yield: 8 servings

Ingredients
1 cup of plain yogurt (250 g)
2 tablespoons of lemon juice (30 ml)
3 cloves of garlic, minced (9 g)
1 medium onion, finely chopped (110 g)
1/2 teaspoons of cayenne pepper (1 g)
1/2 teaspoon of ground cumin (1 g)

1/2 teaspoon of paprika (1 g)
1/4 teaspoon of ground cinnamon
1/4 teaspoon of ground turmeric
2.2 pounds of sirloin steak, cut into small cubes (1 kg)
salt and freshly ground black pepper
8 metal skewers

Method

1. Combine the yogurt, lemon juice, minced garlic, onion, and spices together in a non-reactive bowl. Season with salt and pepper to taste.
2. Add your steaks into the bowl and mix well to coat with marinade. Cover and refrigerate for at least 2 hours or preferably overnight.
3. Preheat your grill to high.
4. Thread the beef cubes onto the skewers.
5. Grill the steaks for 4 to 5 minutes on each side or to your desired doneness.
6. Transfer into a serving platter and serve.

Nutritional Information:

Energy - 242 calories
Fat - 7.6 g
Carbohydrates - 4.2 g
Protein - 36.5 g
Sodium - 245 mg

Grilled Chili Lime Chicken Kebabs

This spicy grilled chicken kebab recipe with lime is

perfect for barbecue parties.

Preparation time: 2 hours 10 minutes
Total time: 2 hours 30 minutes
Yield: 8 servings

Ingredients
1/3 cup olive oil (85 ml)
1/4 cup freshly squeezed lime juice (60 ml)
1 medium onion, finely chopped (110 g)
4 garlic cloves, minced (12 g)
1 teaspoon chili powder (2 g)
1/2 teaspoon wholegrain mustard (1 g)
1/2 teaspoon coriander seed, ground (1 g)
2.2 pounds chicken breast fillet, cut into small cubes (1 kg)
salt and freshly ground black pepper

8 metal skewers

Method
1. In a non-reactive bowl, combine the olive oil, lime juice, onion, garlic, chili powder, wholegrain mustard, and coriander. Season with salt and pepper, to taste.
2. Add the chicken and stir to coat. Cover and refrigerate for 2 hours.
3. Preheat your grill to high heat.
4. Thread chicken onto the skewers.
5. Grill for 5-7 minutes on each side or to your desired doneness.
6. Transfer chicken skewers into a serving dish.
7. Serve and enjoy.

Nutritional Information:

Energy - 270 calories

Fat - 13.7 g

Carbohydrates - 2.1 g

Protein - 33.1 g

Sodium - 249 mg

Homemade Jerk Chicken Drumstick

This awesome grilled jerk chicken is so flavorful, it will soon become everyone's favorite!

Preparation time: 2 hours 10 minutes
Total time: 2 hours 30 minutes
Yield: 4 servings

Ingredients
8 chicken drumsticks (about 1 kg)
1/3 cup olive oil (85 ml)
1/4 cup fresh lime juice (60 ml)
2 tablespoons soy sauce (30 ml)
2 shallots, quartered (80 g)
3 large garlic cloves (10 g)
3 Scotch bonnet or habanero chili, stemmed and seeded (5 g)
1 tablespoon brown sugar (15 g)
1 tablespoon fresh thyme leaves (3.5 g)

1/2 teaspoon nutmeg, freshly grated (1 g)
1/2 teaspoon allspice, ground (1 g)
1/2 teaspoon cinnamon, ground (1 g)
1/4 teaspoon salt (1 g)
1/4 teaspoon black pepper, ground (0.5 g)

Method
1. Combine the olive oil, lime juice, soy sauce, shallots, garlic, chili, brown sugar, and thyme in a food processor. Process until smooth.

2. Add the nutmeg, all spice cinnamon, salt and pepper. Pulse 2-3 times. Transfer mixture into a non-reactive bowl.

3. Add chicken drumsticks and toss to coat. Cover and refrigerate for 2 hours.

4. Preheat your grill to medium heat.

5. Grill chicken for 7-10 minutes on each side.

6. Transfer into a serving dish.

7. Serve and enjoy.

Nutritional Information:

Energy - 285 calories
Fat - 15.0 g
Carbohydrates - 8.9 g

Protein - 26.7 g
Sodium - 475 mg

Easy Grilled Rib Eye

This grilled meat recipe made is so delicious. You can also use chicken or fish to replace meat in this recipe.

Preparation Time: 2 hours 10 minutes
Total Time: 2 hours 30 minutes
Yield: 4 servings

Ingredients
1/4 cup of olive oil (60 ml)
2 tablespoons of lemon juice (30 ml)
1/2 teaspoon garlic powder (1 g)
1 tablespoon of fresh rosemary, finely chopped (3.5 g)
1 tablespoon of fresh thyme, finely chopped (3.5 g)
4 (6 oz. or 180 g) rib eye steaks
2 tablespoons peppercorns (20 g)
salt and freshly ground black pepper
cooking oil spray

Method
1. Combine the oil, lemon juice, garlic powder, rosemary, and thyme in a small bowl. Season with salt and pepper, to taste.
2. Add the steaks in the mixture and marinate for at least 2 hours.
3. Preheat your grill to high. Spray grate with oil.
4. Grill the steaks for 5-7 minutes on each side or to your desired doneness.
5. Transfer into a serving dish. Sprinkle with some crushed peppercorns.
6. Serve and enjoy.

Nutritional Information:

Energy - 286 calories
Fat - 14.4 g
Carbohydrates - 3.4 g
Protein - 35.0 g
Sodium - 226 mg

Grilled Italian Salmon Steaks

This grilled salmon steak recipe is so tasty and healthy.

Preparation time: 10 minutes
Total time: 1 hour and 30 minutes
Yield: 4 servings

Ingredients
4 (5 oz. or 150 g) salmon steaks
1/4 cup olive oil (60 ml)
2 tablespoons balsamic vinegar (30 ml)
1 tablespoon honey (20 ml)
1/2 teaspoon of dried Italian seasoning (1 g)
1/4 teaspoon garlic powder (0.5 g)
salt and freshly ground black pepper

Method

1. Combine the olive oil, balsamic vinegar, honey, Italian seasoning, and garlic powder in a non-reactive bowl. Season with salt and pepper to taste.
2. Add the salmon steaks and turn to coat. Cover and refrigerate for at least an hour.
3. Preheat your grill to high.
4. Grill salmon steaks for 5 minutes on each side.
5. Transfer into a serving dish.
6. Serve and enjoy.

Nutritional Information:

Energy - 230 calories
Fat - 14.2 g
Carbohydrates - 4.6 g
Protein - 22.1 g
Sodium - 51 mg

Honey Mustard Grilled Chicken

Impress your loved ones tonight with this scrumptious grilled chicken recipe.

Preparation time: 2 hours 10 minutes
Total time: 2 hours 30 minutes
Yield: 4 servings

Ingredients

4 (8 oz. or 250 g) quartered chicken - leg and thigh
3/4 cup of mayonnaise (180 g)
2 tablespoons honey (40 ml)
2 tablespoons Dijon mustard (30 g)
1 tablespoon Worcestershire sauce (15 ml)
1 teaspoon garlic, minced (3 g)
salt and freshly ground black pepper

Method

1. In a small bowl, combine the mayonnaise, honey, Dijon mustard, Worcestershire sauce, and garlic. Season with salt and pepper, to taste. Mix them thoroughly.
2. In a non-reactive container, pour the marinade onto your chicken. Cover and refrigerate for 1-2 hours to absorb flavors.
3. Preheat your grill or griddle to medium.
4. Grill chicken for 8-10 minutes on each side.
5. Transfer into a serving dish.
6. Serve and enjoy.

Nutritional Information:
Energy - 309 calories
Fat - 19.2 g
Carbohydrates - 13.6 g
Protein - 21.5 g
Sodium - 472 mg

Grilled Korean Chicken Wings

If you want some zing into your grilled chicken wings, try this recipe!

Preparation time: 2 hours 10 minutes
Total time: 2 hours 30 minutes
Yield: 4 servings

Ingredients
2.2 pounds of chicken wings (1 kg)
1/3 cup of soy sauce (85 ml)
1/3 cup of brown sugar (75 g)
1/3 cup of water (85 ml)
2 tablespoons of rice vinegar (30 ml)
2 teaspoons of hot chili paste (10 g)
1 teaspoon of ground ginger (5 g)
1 teaspoon of sesame oil (5 ml)
1/2 teaspoon of onion powder (1 g)
1/2 teaspoon of garlic powder (1 g)

Method

1. Whisk together the soy sauce, brown sugar, water, and rice vinegar in a small saucepan. Bring to a boil over high heat. Reduce heat and simmer for 3 minutes. Remove from heat.
2. Stir in the remaining ingredients except chicken. Allow to cool.
3. Pour the spicy marinade onto your chicken and refrigerate for least 1-2 hours to absorb flavors.
4. Preheat your grill or griddle to medium.
5. Grill the chicken wings for 8-10 minutes on each side.
6. Transfer into a serving dish.
7. Serve and enjoy.

Nutritional Information:
Energy - 258 calories
Fat - 9.2 g
Carbohydrates - 7.6 g
Protein - 33.6 g
Sodium - 514 mg

Grilled Lamb Chops with Wholegrain Mustard

Lamb chops and mustard goes well together. This fantastic recipe will surely satisfy those hungry

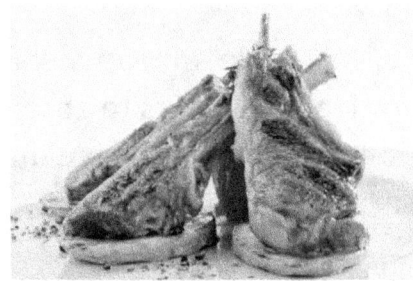

tummies!

Preparation time: 2 hours 10 minutes
Total time: 2 hours 30 minutes
Yield: 8 servings

Ingredients
2.2 pounds lamb chops (1 kg)
6 oz. Greek yogurt (180 g)
1 tablespoon wholegrain mustard (15 g)
2 tablespoons lemon juice (30 ml)
1 tablespoon fresh rosemary, chopped (3.5 g)
1 tablespoon maple syrup (20 ml)
salt and freshly ground black pepper

Method

1. Combine the yogurt, wholegrain mustard, lemon juice, rosemary, and maple syrup in a small bowl. Season with salt and pepper, to taste. Mix well.
2. Pour mixture onto your lamb chops and turn to coat all sides. Cover and refrigerate for at least 1-2 hours to absorb flavors.
3. Preheat your grill or griddle to medium.
4. Grill lamb chops for 5-7 minutes on each side or to your desired doneness.
5. Transfer into a serving dish.
6. Serve and enjoy.

Nutritional Information:

Energy - 236 calories
Fat - 8.8 g
Carbohydrates - 2.9 g
Protein - 34 g
Sodium - 168 mg

Grilled Chicken Legs

A different and easy way to cook your chicken drumsticks!

Preparation time: 2 hours 10 minutes
Total time: 2 hours 30 minutes
Yield: 4 servings

Ingredients
1/2 cup of ketchup (125 g)
2 tablespoons of vegetable oil (30 ml)
2 tablespoons of white wine vinegar (30 ml)
2 tablespoons of Worcestershire sauce (30 ml)
2 tablespoons of brown sugar (30 g)
3 cloves of garlic, chopped (9 g)
1 tablespoon fresh rosemary, chopped (3.5 g)
8 chicken drumsticks (about 2.2 lbs. or 1 kg)
salt and freshly ground black pepper

Method
1. Combine the ketchup, vegetable oil, white wine vinegar, Worcestershire sauce, brown sugar, garlic, and rosemary in a non-reactive bowl.
2. Add the chicken drumsticks and toss to coat. Season with salt and pepper to taste.
3. Preheat your grill to medium heat.
4. Grill chicken drumsticks for 10 minutes on each side or until cooked through.
5. Transfer into a serving dish.
6. Serve and enjoy.

Nutritional Information:

Energy - 277 calories
Fat - 12.5 g
Carbohydrates - 14.8 g
Protein - 26.0 g
Sodium - 440 mg

Grilled Mussels with Basil Pesto

Basil Pesto sauce is not only good for pasta, it can also be used to enhance the flavor of your grilled seafood!

Preparation time: 15 minutes
Total time: 30 minutes
Yield: 8 servings

Ingredients
2.2 pounds mussels, scrubbed and debearded (1 kg)
1 1/2 cups fresh basil leaves, finely chopped (90 g)
3 cloves garlic, minced (9 g)
1/4 cup pine nuts (40 g)
2 tablespoons lemon juice (30 ml)
2 tablespoons parmesan cheese (30 ml)
3/4 cup of olive oil (185 ml)
salt and freshly ground black pepper

Method

1. Steam mussels in a steamer with small amount of water. Discard any unopened mussels. Remove the half shell with no meat.
2. Place the basil, garlic, pine nuts, lemon juice, and parmesan cheese in a blender or food processor. Pulse until it forms a paste.
3. Add the olive oil slowly while the motor is running. Season with salt and pepper, to taste.
4. Spoon pesto sauce over mussels.
5. Preheat your grill to high.
6. Grill mussels for 5-7 minutes.
7. Transfer into a serving platter.
8. Serve and enjoy.

Nutritional Information:

Energy - 249 calories
Fat - 17.9 g
Carbohydrates - 15.4 g
Protein - 15.4 g
Sodium - 432 mg

Chicken Sausage-Filled Squid Skewers

This is definitely not your ordinary squid skewers. The chicken sausage filling complements well with the squid in this wonderful recipe.

Preparation time: 1 hour 10 minutes
Total time: 1 hour 30 minutes
Yield: 4 servings

Ingredients
2 tablespoons of olive oil, divided (30 ml)
1/2 cup of onion, diced (80 g)
1/2 cup of red bell pepper, diced (75 g)
6 ounces (180 g) of chicken sausages, removed from casings, slightly crumbled
1/4 cup of flat-leaf parsley, chopped (15 g)
1 large egg (60 g)
1/8 teaspoon of paprika

8 pieces of medium-sized squid (about 2.2 lbs. or 1 kg)
salt and freshly ground black pepper
8 metal skewers

Method

1. Heat about 1 tablespoon of olive oil in a pan over medium heat. Cook the onion and red pepper in it. Stir and add a pinch of salt. Cook for about 5 minutes. Remove from heat and allow to cool a little.
2. In a bowl, combine the chicken sausage, onion mixture, parsley, egg, paprika, salt, and pepper. Transfer this mixture into a piping bag to pipe into the squid.
3. Pipe the mixture into the calamari. Fill the squid about 2/3 of the way full. Spear the tops of each squid tube with toothpicks to secure the filling. Put the squid on a plate, cover with cling wrap, and refrigerate for about an hour.
4. Preheat your grill to medium-high heat.
5. Brush each squid with the remaining olive oil, coating all sides. Season with some salt and pepper.
6. Grill the stuffed squid, turning occasionally. The stuffing should be cooked through. This should take about 10 to 15 minutes.
7. Transfer into a serving platter.
8. Serve and enjoy.

Nutritional Information:

Energy - 270 calories
Fat - 14.3 g
Carbohydrates - 9.0 g
Protein - 24.9 g
Sodium - 378 mg

Beef Skewers with Teriyaki Sauce

This Asian-inspired grilled skewer recipe goes well with either beef or chicken!

Preparation time: 1 hours 10 minutes
Total time: 1 hour 30 minutes
Yield: 8 servings

Ingredients
2.2 pounds beef sirloin, cut into small pieces (1 kg)
1/4 cup soy sauce (60 ml)
1/4 cup mirin (60 ml)
1/4 cup rice wine vinegar (60 ml)
2 tablespoons brown sugar (30 g)
1 teaspoon ginger juice (5 ml)
2 cloves garlic, minced (6 g)
freshly ground black pepper
wooden skewers

Method
1. In a non-reactive container, mix together the soy sauce, mirin, rice wine vinegar, brown sugar, ginger juice, and garlic.
2. Add the beef and season with pepper to taste. Cover and refrigerate for at least an hour.
3. Thread beef onto the wooden skewers.
4. Preheat your grill to high.
5. Grill the beef skewers for 5 minutes on each side or to your desired doneness. Transfer into a serving platter.
6. Serve and enjoy.

Nutritional Information:
Energy - 243 calories
Fat - 7.1 g
Carbohydrates - 6.7 g
Protein - 35.0 g
Sodium - 590 mg

Korean-Style Rib BBQ

This Korean-style short rib BBQ is totally delicious!

Preparation time: 8 hours 10 minutes
Total time: 8 hours 30 minutes
Yield: 12 servings

Ingredients
3/4 cup of soy sauce (185 ml)
3/4 cup of water (185 ml)
3/4 cup of brown sugar (165 g)
1/4 cup of rice vinegar (60 ml)
1 tablespoon of hot chili paste (15 g)
1 teaspoon of ground ginger (3 g)
1 teaspoon of onion powder (2 g)
1 teaspoon of garlic powder (2 g)
1 teaspoon of sesame oil (5 ml)
4.4 pounds of beef short ribs, trimmed (2 kg)

cooking oil spray

Method
1. Combine the soy sauce, water, brown sugar, and rice vinegar in a saucepan and bring to a boil over high heat. Reduce the heat and let it simmer for about 5 minutes. Remove from heat, add in the chili paste, ginger, onion powder, garlic powder, and sesame oil. Allow to cool.
2. Arrange the ribs in a non-reactive container with lid. Coat the short ribs with marinade and cover the container. Place inside the refrigerator and marinate for 8 hours.
3. Preheat an outdoor grill to medium-high heat and spray grate with oil.
4. Grill the ribs for about 5-7 minutes on each side or to your desired doneness.
5. Transfer into a serving platter.
6. Serve and enjoy.

Nutritional Information:
Energy - 339 calories
Fat - 13.0 g
Carbohydrates - 12.3 g
Protein - 39.9 g
Sodium - 463 mg

Marinated Grilled Shrimp

Shrimp tastes great with even the simplest marinade. You can also try this marinade for grilled meat, chicken,

and fish.

Preparation time: 10 minutes
Total time: 45 minutes
Yield: 8 servings

  Ingredients
1/3 cup of olive oil (85 ml)
2 tablespoons of red wine vinegar (30 ml)
2 tablespoons of fresh dill weed, chopped (7 g)
3 cloves of garlic, minced (9 g)
1/2 teaspoon of cayenne pepper (1 g)
2.2 pounds of fresh shrimp, peeled and deveined (1 kg)
salt and freshly ground black pepper
cooking oil spray
wooden skewers

Method

1. Mix together the olive oil, red wine vinegar, dill, garlic, and cayenne pepper in a non-reative bowl. Season with the salt and pepper to taste.
2. Add the shrimps. Toss to coat. Cover and refrigerate for 30 minutes.
3. Preheat your grill or griddle to medium-high heat.
4. Thread the shrimps onto the skewers. Spray the grill grate with oil.
5. Grill the shrimp for 2 to 3 minutes on each side.
6. Transfer into a serving platter.
7. Serve and enjoy.

Tip: Serve grilled shrimps with fresh green salad to complete the meal.

Nutritional Information:

Energy - 194 calories
Fat - 8.3 g
Carbohydrates - 2.6 g
Protein - 26.1 g
Sodium - 426 mg

Grilled Beef Bratwurst

You can use different spices to enhance the flavor of these grilled sausages.

Preparation time: 10 minutes
Total time: 15 minutes
Yield: 4 servings

Ingredients
4 (3.5 oz. or 100 g) bratwurst sausages
1 medium onion, thinly sliced (110 g)
2 tablespoons of butter (30 g)
1/4 teaspoon paprika (0.5 g)

Method
1. Gently prick the bratwurst with a fork. Place the sausages into a pan with the onion slices and butter.

2. Cook the sausage and onions for 10 minutes over medium heat. Remove from heat.

3. Preheat grill to medium-high heat.

4. Grill the bratwurst for 10-12 minutes. Turning occasionally to distribute the heat evenly.

5. Transfer into a serving dish.

6. Serve and enjoy.

Nutritional Information:

Energy - 202 calories
Fat - 12.8 g
Carbohydrates - 8.7 g
Protein - 14.4 g
Sodium - 662 mg

Ultimate Chicken Barbecue

This recipe has the best marinade for chicken barbecue. So simple and easy to make!

Preparation time: 2 hours 10 minutes
Total time: 2 hours 30 minutes
Yield: 8 servings

Ingredients
1/3 cup ketchup (85 g)
1/3 cup brown sugar (75 g)
1/3 cup soy sauce (85 ml)
1 tablespoon Worcestershire sauce (15 ml)
1 teaspoon garlic powder (2 g)
1 teaspoon onion powder (2 g)
1 tablespoon hot pepper sauce (15 ml)
1/2 teaspoon cumin, ground (1 g)
1/2 teaspoon paprika (1 g)
2.2 pounds chicken thighs (1 kg)
2 cups cherry tomatoes (300 g)
8 metal skewers

Method
1. Mix together the ketchup, brown sugar, soy sauce, Worcestershire sauce, garlic powder, onion powder, hot pepper sauce, cumin, and paprika in a small bowl.
2. Combine half of the marinade and the chicken thighs in a non-reactive container. Mix well. Cover and refrigerate for 2 hours.
3. Thread chicken and cherry tomatoes alternately onto the skewers.
4. Preheat grill to medium heat.
5. Grill the chicken kebab for 10-12 minutes or until cooked through. Turning occasionally to distribute the heat evenly. Brush with remaining marinade frequently.
6. Transfer into a serving dish.
7. Serve and enjoy.

Nutritional Information:

Energy - 265 calories
Fat - 8.6 g
Carbohydrates - 11.8 g
Protein - 30.7 g
Sodium - 583 mg

Spicy Grilled Steaks

If you are looking for a grilled steak recipe with a mild kick, this is the recipe for you!

Preparation Time: 2 hours 10 minutes
Total Time: 2 hours 30 minutes
Yield: 2 servings

Ingredients
2 tablespoons of lime juice (30 ml)
2 tablespoons of olive oil (30 ml)
2 cloves of garlic, minced (6 g)
1/2 teaspoon of cayenne pepper (1 g)
1/4 teaspoon of paprika (0.5 g)
1/4 teaspoon cumin (0.5 g)
2 (5 oz. or 150 g) sirloin steaks
salt and freshly ground black pepper, to taste

Method
1. Mix together the olive oil, lime juice, garlic, cayenne pepper, paprika, and cumin in a small bowl. Season with salt and pepper, to taste.
2. Place the steaks in a non-reactive container with lid and pour the marinade over them. Turn to coat all sides of the steaks. Cover with a lid and refrigerate for at least 2 hours.
3. Preheat your grill for high heat.
4. Grill each side of the steaks for 5-7 minutes on each side or to your desired doneness.
5. Transfer into in a serving dish.
6. Serve and enjoy.

Nutritional Information:

Energy - 275 calories
Fat - 14.2 g
Carbohydrates - 1.0 g
Protein - 34.6 g
Sodium - 223 mg

Chipotle Garlic Lamb Chops

A flavorful recipe for grilled lamb chops.

Preparation time: 2 hours 10 minutes
Total time: 2 hours 30 minutes
Yield: 8 servings (2 pieces each)

Ingredients
8 lamb chops (about 3 lbs. or 1.4 kg)
1/2 cup ketchup (125 g)
1/2 cup maple syrup (160 g)
2 tablespoons olive oil (30 ml)
2 tablespoons soy sauce (30 ml)
1 tablespoon Worcestershire sauce (15 ml)
1 teaspoon garlic, chopped (3 g)
2 chipotle chilies, minced (5 g)

Method

1. In a non-reactive bowl, combine the ketchup, maple syrup, olive oil, soy sauce, Worcestershire sauce, garlic, and chipotle chilies. Mix well.
2. Add the lamb chops and turn to coat all sides. Cover and refrigerate for 2 hours.
3. Preheat your grill to medium heat.
4. Grill the lamb chops for 5 minutes on each side or to your desired doneness.
5. Transfer into a serving dish.
6. Serve and enjoy.

Nutritional Information:

Energy - 259 calories
Fat - 9.8 g
Carbohydrates - 17.8 g
Protein - 24.4 g
Sodium - 480 mg

Easy Grilled Squid

This is a super easy and tasty grilled squid recipe!

Preparation time: 35 minutes
Total time: 45 minutes
Yield: 8 servings

Ingredients

2.2 pounds of medium-sized squid, cleaned (1 kg)
1/4 cup soy sauce (60 ml)
1/4 cup brown sugar (75 g)
2 tablespoons lime juice (30 ml)
1 tablespoon Worcestershire sauce (15 ml)
1 teaspoon garlic, minced (3 g)
1/2 teaspoon freshly ground black pepper (1 g)

Method

1. Combine the soy sauce, sugar, lime juice, Worcestershire sauce, and garlic in a medium bowl.

2. Add the squid and season with pepper to taste. Mix well. Let sit for 30 minutes to absorb flavors.
3. Preheat grill to medium-high.
4. Grill the squid for 5 minutes on each side or until just cooked.
5. Transfer into a serving dish.
6. Serve and enjoy.

Nutritional Information:

Energy - 158 calories
Fat - 4.5 g
Carbohydrates - 9.2 g
Protein - 18.6 g
Sodium - 521 mg

Citrus-Marinated Grilled Chicken Breasts

Absolutely delicious, just what you need for an outdoor barbecue party.

Preparation time: 2 hours 10 minutes
Total time: 2 hours 30 minutes
Yield: 4 servings

Ingredients

1/2 cup of orange juice (125 ml)
1 tablespoon of honey (20 ml)
1 tablespoon of fresh cilantro, chopped (3.5 g)
1 teaspoon orange zest, finely grated (5 g)
1 teaspoon paprika (2 g)
4 (6 oz. or 180 g) boneless and skinless chicken breast
cooking oil spray

Method

1. Combine the orange juice, honey, cilantro, zest, and paprika in a bowl. Transfer to a resealable bag with the chicken. Seal the bag. Shake to coat chicken with marinade evenly. Marinate in the fridge for at least an hour.
2. Preheat your grill or griddle to medium-high heat. Spray the grill grate with oil.
3. Grill chicken for about 7 minutes on each side or until cooked through.
4. Transfer into a serving platter.
5. Serve and enjoy.

Nutritional Information:

Energy - 220 calories
Fat - 9.7 g
Carbohydrates - 8.0 g
Protein - 24.1 g
Sodium - 205 mg

Grilled Lamb Chops with Herbs

This is a simple recipe for grilled lamb chops with herbs.

Preparation Time: 10 minutes
Total Time: 20 minutes
Yield: 8 servings (2 pieces each)

Ingredients
1/4 cup of olive oil (60 ml)
1/4 cup of red wine vinegar (60 ml)
1 tablespoon of fresh parsley, chopped (3.5 g)
1 tablespoon of fresh thyme, chopped (3.5 g)
2 cloves of garlic, peeled and minced (6 g)
8 lamb chops (about 3 lbs. or 1.4 kg)
salt and freshly ground black pepper

Method

1. Combine the olive oil, red wine vinegar, parsley, thyme, and garlic in a medium glass bowl.
2. Add the lamb chops and turn to coat all sides. Season with salt and pepper to taste. Let sit for 30 minutes to absorb flavors.
3. Preheat your grill to high.
4. Grill the lamb chops on the grill for 5 minutes on each side or to your desired doneness.
5. Transfer into a serving platter.
6. Serve and enjoy.

Nutritional Information:

Energy - 294 calories
Fat - 20.7 g
Carbohydrates - 0.6 g
Protein - 25.5 g
Sodium - 201 mg

Shish Kabobs

Ground lamb is the star of this easy-to-make Middle-Eastern kabob recipe!

Preparation time: 10 minutes
Total time: 20 minutes
Yield: 8 servings

Ingredients
2.2 pounds of lean ground lamb (1 kg)
2 medium onions, chopped finely (220 g)
1/4 cup of fresh mint leaves, chopped finely (15 g)
2 tablespoons of fresh cilantro, chopped finely (7 g)
1 tablespoon of ginger paste (15 g)
1 teaspoon of green chili paste (5 g)
1/2 teaspoon of ground cumin (1 g)
1/2 teaspoon of ground coriander (1 g)
1/2 teaspoon of paprika (1 g)
1/2 teaspoon of cayenne pepper (1 g)
1/4 teaspoon of Kosher salt (1 g)

8 metal skewers

Method

1. Combine the ground lamb, onions, mint, cilantro, ginger paste, chili paste, and the rest of the seasonings/spices. Place in the chiller for 1-2 hours.

2. Take a ball of ground lamb in one hand and form a sausage around a skewer. Repeat with the rest of the lamb. Refrigerate again until you are ready to grill them.

3. Preheat your grill or griddle to high. Spray the grate with oil.

4. Put the kabobs on the grill. Cook for about 15 minutes. Turning halfway through cooking to cook all sides.

5. Transfer into a serving dish.

6. Serve and enjoy.

Nutritional Information:

Energy - 229 calories
Fat - 8.6 g
Carbohydrates - 3.7 g
Protein - 32.4 g
Sodium - 170 mg

Grilled Salmon with Lemon and Thyme

A simple grilled salmon recipe made flavorful with the addition of lemon and thyme.

Preparation time: 5 minutes
Total time: 15 minutes
Yield: 4 servings

Ingredients
1/4 cup of lemon juice (60 ml)
2 tablespoons melted butter (30 g)
1 teaspoon lemon zest, finely grated (3.5 g)
2 tablespoons fresh thyme, chopped (7 g)
4 (5 oz. or 150 g) salmon fillets
salt and freshly ground black pepper

cooking oil spray

Method
1. Mix together lemon juice, butter, zest, and thyme in a medium bowl.
2. Add the salmon fillets and turn to coat all sides. Season with salt and pepper to taste. Let sit for a few minutes to absorb flavors
3. Preheat your grill or griddle to high. Spray the grate with oil.
4. Grill salmon for 5 minutes on each side or until just cooked.
5. Transfer into a serving dish.
6. Serve and enjoy.

Nutritional Information:

Energy - 210 calories
Fat - 13.1 g
Carbohydrates - 1.5 g
Protein - 22.3 g
Sodium - 242 mg

Spicy Grilled Lobster

This spicy grilled lobster recipe is also can be used in other seafood, fish, or poultry.

Preparation Time: 5 minutes
Total Time: 15 minutes
Yield: 4 servings

Ingredients
1/4 cup of olive oil (60 ml)
2 tablespoons of lemon juice (30 ml)
1 tablespoon Worcestershire sauce (15 ml)
1/2 teaspoon of garlic powder (1 g)
1/4 teaspoon of white pepper (0.5 g)
4 (4 oz. or 120 g) lobster tails, cleaned
salt and freshly ground black pepper
cooking oil spray

Method
1. Preheat your grill to high.
2. In a small bowl, combine the olive oil, lemon juice, Worcestershire sauce, garlic powder, and white pepper. Cut the lobster tails in half, lengthwise. Brush with marinade. Spray the grill grate with oil.
3. Put the lobster tails, flesh side down, on the grill and grill for 10 to 12 minutes. Turn once. Baste with marinade frequently.
4. Transfer into a serving dish.
5. Serve and enjoy.

Nutritional Information:

Energy - 198 calories
Fat - 11.5 g
Carbohydrates - 1.2 g
Protein - 21.7 g
Sodium - 741 mg

Sweet and Spicy Grilled Tuna Belly

A sweet and spicy take on the all-time favorite grilled tuna belly!

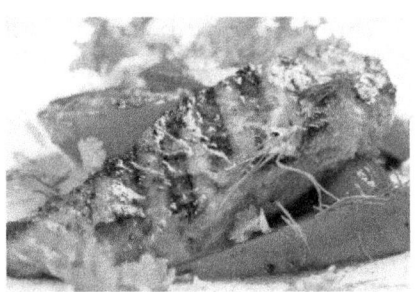

Preparation time: 2 hour 10 minutes
Total time: 2 hours 30 minutes
Yield: 4 servings

Ingredients
1 pound tuna belly (450 g)
1/2 cup ketchup (125 g)
1/4 cup soy sauce (60 ml)
1/4 cup brown sugar (55 g)
2 tablespoons vegetable oil (30 ml)
1 tablespoon Worcestershire sauce (15 ml)
1 tablespoon chili paste (15 g)
1 teaspoon sweet paprika (2 g)
1/2 teaspoon cumin, ground (1 g)
1/2 teaspoon coriander, ground (1 g)
salt and freshly ground black pepper

Method
1. Combine the ketchup, brown sugar, soy sauce, vegetable oil, Worcestershire sauce, chili paste, paprika, cumin, and coriander in a medium glass bowl. Season with salt and pepper, to taste. Mix well.
2. Add the tuna belly and turn to coat all sides. Cover and refrigerate for 2 hours.
3. Preheat your grill to high. Spray the grill grate with oil.
4. Grill tuna belly for 5-7 minutes on each side or until just cooked.
5. Transfer into a serving dish.
6. Serve and enjoy.

Nutritional information:

Energy - 259 calories
Fat - 8.7 g
Carbohydrates - 17.2 g
Protein - 27.7 g
Sodium - 552 mg

Spiced Shrimp Skewers with Garlic and Herb

This mildly spiced shrimp skewer recipe is a sure hit!

Preparation time: 10 minutes
Total time: 30 minutes
Yield: 4 servings (2 skewers each)

Ingredients
1 pound medium shrimps, peeled (450 g)
1/4 cup olive oil (60 ml)
2 tablespoons lime juice (30 ml)
1 teaspoon sweet paprika (2 g)
1 teaspoon cumin, ground (2 g)
1 teaspoon garlic, chopped (2 g)
2 tablespoons fresh parsley, chopped (7 g)
salt and freshly ground black pepper
8 wooden skewers

Method

1. Combine the olive oil, lime juice, paprika, cumin, and garlic in a glass bowl.
2. Add the shrimps and toss to coat. Season with salt and pepper, to taste. Let sit for a few minutes.
3. Preheat your grill or griddle to high. Spray the grill grate with oil.
4. Grill for 3 minutes on each side or until just cooked. Turn once.
5. Transfer into a serving dish.
6. Serve and enjoy.

Nutritional information:

Energy - 222 calories
Fat - 14.2 g
Carbohydrates - 1.1 g
Protein - 24.6 g
Sodium - 306 mg

Homemade Grilled Pizza

Create something different using your grill with this awesome grilled pizza recipe!

Preparation time: 2 hours 10 minutes
Total time: 2 hours 45 minutes
Yield: 4 servings

Ingredients

Crust:
1 package of active dry yeast (7 g)
1 cup of warm water (250 ml)
A pinch of white sugar (2 g)
2 teaspoons of salt (10 g)
1 tablespoon of olive oil (15 ml)
3 1/3 cups of flour (420 g)
2 cloves of garlic, minced (6 g)
1 teaspoon of dried oregano (2 g)

Pizza:
2/3 cup of tomato sauce (165 g)
1 cup of cherry tomatoes, halved (150 g)

6 oz. (180 g) turkey ham, chopped
1/4 cup of green bell peppers, thinly sliced (40 g)
1 cup of shredded mozzarella cheese (125 g)
1/4 cup of chopped fresh basil (15 g)
salt and freshly ground black pepper

Method
1. Dissolve the yeast in warm water and add in the sugar. Let it sit for 10 minutes. Add in the salt, olive oil, and the flour. Mix well.
2. Place dough into a floured work area and knead until smooth. Place in an oiled bowl and cover with a wet cloth. Allow to rise for about 1 hour. Knead in the garlic and oregano. Let it rise for another hour.
3. Preheat your grill to medium-high.
4. Divide the dough in half and make a pizza crust with each half.
5. Place one crust on the grill. Cook until golden, turn the dough over to cook the other side. Remove from heat.
6. Spread tomato sauce over the pie crusts. Add the toppings and sprinkle mozzarella cheese and basil. Return the pizza to the grill and cover. Cook until the cheese melts.
7. Transfer into a serving dish.
8. Serve immediately and enjoy.

Nutritional information:

Energy - 339 calories
Fat - 5.2 g
Carbohydrates - 58.1 g
Protein - 14.4 g
Sodium - 709 mg

Grilled Vegetables with Herbs

This wonderful grilled vegetable recipe with herbs makes a perfect side to your grilled meat or poultry.

Preparation Time: 10 minutes
Total Time: 30 minutes
Yield: 8 servings

Ingredients
1/2 cup of extra virgin olive oil (125 ml)
1/4 cup balsamic vinegar (60 ml)
1/2 teaspoon garlic powder (1 g)
1/4 cup fresh mixed herbs, chopped (15 g)
2 medium zucchini, cut into 1/2-inch slices (400 g)
2 medium eggplant, cut into 1/2-inch slices (400 g)
1 pound of baby potatoes (450 g)
4 medium tomatoes (500 g)
salt and freshly ground black pepper

cooking oil spray

Method
1. Preheat your grill or griddle to medium-high. Spray the grate with oil spray.
2. Combine olive oil, balsamic vinegar, herbs, and garlic powder in a large glass bowl.
3. Add the vegetables and toss to coat. Season with salt and pepper to taste.
4. Grill vegetables, turning as needed to cook all sides. Brush with marinade occasionally.
5. Transfer into a serving dish.
6. Serve and enjoy.

Nutritional information:

Energy - 160 calories
Fat - 9.1 g
Carbohydrates - 19.6 g
Protein - 4.0 g
Sodium - 114 mg

Grilled Carrot and Asparagus

Nutritious and very yummy. You're bound to enjoy the Mediterranean taste of this grilled asparagus and carrots.

Preparation time: 10 minutes
Total time: 20 minutes
Yield: 6 servings

Ingredients
1 pound of fresh asparagus, trimmed (450 g)
1 pound of carrot, peeled (450 g)
1/2 cup of extra virgin olive oil (125 ml)
1/4 cup red wine vinegar (60 ml)
1/2 teaspoon Italian seasoning (1 g)
salt and freshly ground black pepper

Method
1. Preheat your grill or griddle to medium-high. Spray the grate with oil spray.
2. Combine olive oil, red wine vinegar, and Italian seasoning in a large glass bowl.
3. Add the asparagus and carrots. Toss to coat. Season with salt and pepper to taste.
4. Grill vegetables, turning as needed to cook all sides. Brush with marinade occasionally.
5. Place in a serving dish.
6. Serve and enjoy.

Nutritional information:

Energy - 121 calories
Fat - 8.6 g
Carbohydrates - 10.5 g
Protein - 2.3 g
Sodium - 151 mg

Easy Corn Kabobs

This corn kabobs is the perfect side to your meat or chicken barbecue!

Preparation time: 10 minutes
Total time: 25 minutes
Yield: 4 servings

Ingredients
1/4 cup of olive oil (60 ml)
1/4 cup of lime juice (60 ml)
2 tablespoons taco seasoning mix (7 g)
4 ears of corn, cut into 1-inch pieces (800 g)
vegetables of your choice, the ones that go well with kabobs

Method
1. Mix together the oil, lime juice, and taco seasoning mix in a large glass bowl.

2. Add the vegetables and corn. Toss to coat.
3. Preheat grill to medium-high.
4. Thread the vegetables and corn alternately onto the skewers.
5. Grill for about 10-15 minutes, or until the vegetables are tender, turning as needed. Brush with marinade frequently.
6. Place in a serving platter.
7. Serve and enjoy.

Nutritional information:

Energy - 182 calories
Fat - 15.6 g
Carbohydrates - 20.5 g
Protein - 3.3 g
Sodium - 165 mg

Grilled Mixed Veggies

A fantastic side to your grilled meat, fish, or poultry!

Preparation time: 10 minutes
Total time: 25 minutes
Yield: 6 servings

Ingredients
1/3 cup of olive oil (85 ml)
2 tablespoons of balsamic vinegar (30 ml)
1/2 teaspoon of salt (2.5 g)
1/2 teaspoon of black pepper, ground (1 g)
2 eggplants, cut into 1/2-inch slices (400 g)
2 zucchinis, cut into 1/2-inch slices (400 g)
2 bell peppers, cut into 1/2-inch slices (240 g)

Method
1. Combine the olive oil, soy sauce, balsamic vinegar, salt, and pepper in a large glass bowl.

2. Put all of the veggies into the marinade and let sit for a few minutes.
3. Preheat grill or griddle to medium-high.
4. Grill vegetables for bout 10-15 minutes, or until the vegetables are tender, turning as needed. Brush with marinade frequently.
5. Transfer into a serving platter.
6. Serve and enjoy.

Nutritional information:

Energy - 170 calories
Fat - 9.2 g
Carbohydrates - 22.6 g
Protein - 4.3 g
Sodium - 210 mg

www.ingramcontent.com/pod-product-compliance
Lightning Source LLC
Chambersburg PA
CBHW071437070526
44578CB00001B/110